MOON MAN

MOON MAN

The True Story of
a Filmmaker on the CIA Hit List

BART
SIBREL

Sibrel.com

MOON MAN
The True Story of
a Filmmaker on the CIA Hit List

Sibrel.com
Washington, D.C.
USA

First Published in the United States of America 2021

Cataloguing-in-Publication Data
A CIP record for this book is available from the Library of Congress.

ISBN 978-1-5136-8656-1

Sibrel.com

In memory of the Chief of Security
where the first Moon Landing was filmed

About the Author

Bart Sibrel has been a filmmaker and writer for most of his life. He is an award winning filmmaker, writer, and investigative journalist who has been producing television programs and documentaries for over thirty-five years. Sibrel has owned five video production companies, been employed by two of the three major networks, worked as a television news reporter, and has produced segments for ABC, NBC, CBS, and CNN. Articles featuring Sibrel's films have been published in *The New York Times, USA Today, The Washington Post,* and *Time magazine.* His awards from the American Motion Picture Society include Best Cinematography, Best Editing, and Top Ten Director.

Born in 1965 Bart Sibrel grew up as the biggest fan of the purported Moon landings, it wasn't until he was a teenager that he began to look more closely at these events and even then it took him another ten years to become fully convinced of their unfortunate falsification. Sibrel considers that a patriotic attachment to the emotional event of human beings travelling to the Moon has created a collective cognitive dissonance that still prevents most people from waking up to the deplorable reality behind the propaganda.

Contents

Introduction

This is the story of the man who was punched in the face by astronaut Edwin "Buzz" Aldrin after I called him "a liar, a coward, and a thief." The pages that follow will detail exactly why I came to say such harsh things to the man who was once my most admired hero.

One day, in the course of my filmmaking and writing work, I met an elderly gentleman who worked as a contractor for NASA during the days of the Apollo space program in the 1960s. He told me plainly that the Moon missions were falsified by the CIA. He explained that this was done in order to promote positive domestic morale during the Nixon administration's notoriously unsuccessful and highly protested Vietnam War. It was policy to temporarily bluff the Soviet Union into thinking that the United States' rocket technology was superior to theirs, specifically because the exact opposite was true.

When the first lunar landing was said to have occurred I was four years old and sleeping quietly in bed, oblivious to the future controversy which awaited me. In fact, I grew up as a great fan of the Moon missions, having a dozen or so cherished pictures of them on my bedroom wall. I gazed at my prized pictures every day, from the age of four to fourteen, before I even considered the *possibility* of their falsification. Ten years of brainwashing was certainly going to be a lot to overcome. The very idea of the missions being government propaganda came by way of a NASA contractor, William (Bill) Kaysing. He was a technical writer at Rockedyne in California and held high level security status at the company. When I first saw him during an appearance on television as a fourteen-year old, espousing the US government's deception with one hundred percent certainty as a first-hand eyewitness, I was fortunate that the concept caught me as an open-minded young teenager. After the TV program I went over to the pictures on my bedroom wall and saw, for the very first time, those anomalies in these photographs of which he spoke. Discrepancies I had somehow overlooked for a decade, though they were right in front of my eyes, hidden in plain sight under the trance of scientific grandeur and blind patriotism. Like a perplexing optical illusion that had to be explained to me, the fake backdrops began to appear right before my previously wide-shut eyes. "Huh" I said to myself, and the seed of the truth was planted. Thank you Bill Kaysing.

Ten years later, as it turned out, the twenty-four-year-old filmmaker that I had become was editing a video for the very man who had produced the program in which Kaysing had appeared. I asked my client for the name of this man whom he had interviewed a decade ago, the one who so confidently declared that the Moon landings were a clever government deception. But unfortunately, this television producer did not remember the man's name. He did however direct me to the production company that had made the program. I telephoned them and they informed me to my astonishment, that had I called just a day later, I would have never been able to find out who or where this man was, as they were in the process of throwing out all archived materials that were over ten years old to make room for more recent projects.

I remember first calling Bill Kaysing from a pay telephone just across the street from where I lived and worked, in case they really did fake the Moon missions and had substituted this whistleblower with a proxy in order to entrap those investigating such matters. After a few seconds of talking with him, I quickly discerned that he was the genuine article, probably because of his matter-of-fact folksy and grandfatherly demeanor. This conversation eventually led to a lengthy investigation into the matter, and finally, though several years later, to the production of my documentary film on the subject, titled *A Funny Thing Happened on the way to the* Moon. That project led to the follow-up piece two years later called *Astronauts Gone Wild*, in which I asked several Apollo astronauts on camera to swear on a Bible that their missions were authentic, in the process of which I was infamously punched in the face by Buzz Aldrin, and unceremoniously kicked in the butt by astronaut Ed Mitchell. Incredibly, I also unintentionally recorded secret audio of an Apollo astronaut discussing with his son whether to have me "whacked" (murdered) by the CIA. The voice on the actual recording said, "Do you want me to call the CIA and have him whacked?" Surely plotting my assassination would not be necessary if the USA really had landed a man on the Moon and I was just a crazy conspiracy theorist, rather than an investigative journalist who had just stumbled upon a genuine and outrageous government deception.

Have you ever wondered about the claim to have travelled to and walked on the Moon in 1969, on the very *first* attempt, even though right here on Earth Mt. Everest and the South Pole took *numerous* tries before achieving success? We allegedly accomplished this amazing feat with very primitive technology (a modern day cell phone has one *million* times more computing power than *all* that NASA was able to access back then). Yet over five decades later, despite all the advancements in space hardware and computers, the farthest that astronauts can travel from the Earth is only *one-thousandth* the distance to the Moon.

If forty two years after Lindbergh first flew solo across the Atlantic ocean men were walking on the Moon, then fifty years after accomplishing Moon travel shouldn't there be visitors travelling at the very least deep into the solar system by now? Rocket scientists expected human crews on Mars ten years after landing on the Moon, but that didn't happen. And shouldn't there be many international bases on the Moon by now, when of course as we all know, there are none?

Every genuine technological achievement in the history of the world, such as the automobile, the airplane, or nuclear power, has been duplicated by others and over the decades technically surpassed the initial breakthrough. Yet this is not the case for manned space travel. In the knowledge that it is impossible for technology to go backwards, the fact that today, despite some five decades worth of more advanced technology, NASA can only send astronauts into low-Earth orbit, rather than to lunar orbit and landing, as was claimed over *half a century* ago, then the only conclusion that is left, however sad and horrific, is that the claims of the 1960s were falsified.

Governments have lied and used false propaganda on numerous prior occasions, so this should not actually surprise anyone. Yet it is a difficult pill to swallow. During the incredible civil unrest caused by the highly unpopular Vietnam War, a successful lunar landing in 1969 would give the American public something most needed to cheer about. The only way to ensure success and not risk killing the crews on live television during the most dangerous untried mission of all time, *which is still unachievable today*, was simply to stage it, like a clever bluff in poker.

If I told you that Toyota had invented a car fifty years ago, with five decades older technology, that could go fifty thousand miles on one gallon of gasoline, yet today their best car can only go fifty miles per gallon (one-thousandth the distance), would you not laugh at the preposterousness of the fifty-year old claim? Therefore, the fraudulent nature of this long-ago Moon landing claim is equally obvious. If it were not for people's attachment to the emotionally-charged event of the alleged Moon landings, they would easily see the truth of this fraud. Instead, telling people the truth is like taking candy away from a child.

Yes, I am the reluctant "Moon Man" who was punched in the face by Buzz Aldrin. As you read through the following pages you will discover exactly why I came to say such harsh things to the man who was once my hero. While I proceed to show exactly who, what, when, where, why, and how the Apollo missions were staged, on the advice of a good friend, I will also describe the way all of this has dramatically affected my life – personally, professionally, and spiritually – in ways that you might not imagine and in ways that I could never have foretold.

The overriding reason why I am pursuing this matter so relentlessly is because the moment I realized that this major event was falsified, I felt compelled to bring this historic deception into the light.

"The bitterest truth,
is better than the sweetest lie."

– *Men in Black 3*

Chapter One

A Funny Thing Happened
on the Way to the Moon

To put the following into context it would be helpful to watch a three minute video of my summary of this matter, and then my documentary *A Funny Thing Happened on the Way to the Moon*, so you will best understand what I am about to describe and provide context. Please go to **Sibrel.com** and click on the *Moon Man* links **#1** and **#2**.

Believe it or not, the Wright Brothers, Neil Armstrong, and myself, were all born in and around that all-American town of Dayton Ohio, possibly the most representative state of American culture in the entire nation and generally considered to be the most critical swing state of nearly all presidential elections. In fact, I was born at aviation's highly acclaimed and secretive Wright-Patterson Air Force Base, which is located there. My father was a high-ranking officer in the United States Air Force. I grew up, from the moment of my birth, surrounded by the latest and greatest that aerospace had to offer.

My favorite aircraft was, and still is, the impressive Lockheed SR-71 dubbed the "Blackbird". Developed by the secretive Skunk Works, a military department of the aerospace company Lockheed Martin, this supersonic, high-flying top secret (at the time) aircraft was capable of flying at nearly 2500 miles per hour (4000 kph). It was used for taking highly-sensitive aerial reconnaissance photographs of Soviet military bases, among other targets. The titanium mechanical bird flew like a dream with the cleanest burning airplane engines that I have ever seen, even to this day. And at 85,000 feet, (25,900 meters, 16 miles), the two-seater Blackbird flew to the highest altitude humanly and technologically possible without actually being called a spacecraft. It was from this incredible vantage point that satellite-like espionage pictures were taken, and some believe that the technological maverick is still in use today.

Secrecy in the Air Force is as common as French fries at McDonalds. To this day my father holds the details of very many secrets which he plans on taking to the grave with him. Some may have to do with the CIA overthrowing democratically elected governments (including that of the USA), some may have to do with elaborate weather modification technology used as a weapon of war, and some may even have to do with the lunar landing fraud itself. We will never know.

At the time of the alleged first steps on the Moon I was fast asleep in bed, no doubt dreaming of walking on the Moon myself. Like many school children at the time, I was enamored with space travel through the constant barrage of toys and television programs with this theme. In fact, the *Star Trek* series came along just prior to the purported Moon missions, perhaps designed in part to help win over the public to the plausibility of space travel. Agencies like the CIA have been churning out television programs and films with Hollywood's cooperation since the early 1950s in an attempt to control public opinion. Today the term "Predictive Programming" is used to describe the psychological tactic of emotionally imprinting a concept through media arts in order for the masses to accept the future perceived reality of what they are being programmed to believe as real, even though it is not, through fictionalized television and cinema. As Founding Father and President John Adams said, when addressing the future generations of American citizens,

> You will never know how much it cost the present Generation to preserve your Freedom! I hope you will make good use of it. If you do not, I shall repent in Heaven that I ever took half the Pains to preserve it.[1]

Like most Americans, I grew up accepting the authenticity of the Moon landings as second nature. I was brought up believing these events to be real was good for the world, good for America, good for me, and made all of American industry and science good as well. To have to conclude that it was all a CIA deception, which I now believe it unfortunately most assuredly was, removes all of that embellished glory, and substitutes criminal deceit in its place.

It is a most painful and mournful process to admit this deplorable truth. Few are willing to do the same in pursuit of honor and principle. This is because believing that you will win the lottery, even though you really know that you won't, is a pleasurable fantasy, and who wants to pass on getting pleasure? Disclosing the deplorable truth about this subject is like telling a fan of the team that won the Super Bowl that they only did so by cheating. Even though it's true, people are ready to punch you in the face for saying so. They might even admit the fact that they have no genuine interest in knowing the truth, because they would rather believe an inspiring lie than the despicable truth.

Seeing how elements of the US government agencies were awarded an equivalent of nearly two hundred billion dollars in today's currency, for the privilege of lying to their own fellow Americans (and to the rest of the world) the reality behind the façade that was the Apollo missions, discovering that it was all a show, is like buying an expensive new car and then finding out that it's actually ten years old, has had four owners, and that the title is still in someone else's name.

Personally, if I had cancer and was terminally ill, I would want to know. Wouldn't you? I think the majority of people would answer "yes" if given time to deeply consider such news, yet there are those in powerful positions that seem to think the exact opposite. Proof of the accuracy of this belief of mine is the fact that eighty percent of people who have watched my documentary A Funny Thing... who previously believed that the Moon landings were genuine, reverse their opinion after viewing my film. This is remarkable, and it is precisely why the film has never been broadcast, though several different networks have purchased the rights to do so over the years, yet each and every time they have chickened out, or have been told not to televise it by executive superiors at the eleventh hour.

On one occasion I was in conversation with the head of the aerospace department at a prestigious university, and this college professor told me plainly that even if he saw one of the Apollo astronauts confess on national television that the Moon missions were falsified, he would *still* think that the missions were real! Can you believe that? This is a fantastic example of cognitive dissonance. This man cannot alter his opinion on this matter because the effect of so doing would in turn alter so much of his personal worldview that he would find it too immeasurably difficult to cope with. What arrogance for him to think that he could know more about the matter than a first-hand Apollo astronaut eyewitness! In my opinion, this is the dangerous condition of pride, and it is everywhere. Pride prohibits the plainest of truths from being seen.

This is the sort of thing I am up against, a citizenry perpetually asleep and collectively dreaming an immorally contrived, grandiose, corrupt, government agency-driven delusion. Nor do such citizens wish to be woken up to the stark reality of their scandalously-hypnotized state, so they resist and ridicule all those who, like myself, are trying to stop them from sleepwalking off the edge of the cliff.

Additionally, when those in the mainstream media at mid-management level attempt to show the nation at large this grievous Moon landing deception of their leaders through the established channels of supposed "news", the powers-that-be above them, who are directly manipulated by the tentacles of this dark federal government control, refuse to broadcast or publish anything that would bring about the demise of their own unscrupulous system, either because they are directly profiting from it, or because they are being coerced into conforming to it. I suppose that this is the logical result of putting the foxes in charge of the henhouse. The question then arises, what can be done about this sad and unjust state of governmental agency and media affairs? We need only to take a look at history for the answer.

As even Solomon, the wisest man who ever lived, said that there was "nothing new under the sun," it has been said by noted historians that not only does history repeat itself, the cycle of instituted governments repeats itself as well. They always begin with the sincerest intentions of individual liberty, inspired by a citizenry fleeing an oppressive leadership who are therefore establishing a new government in its place that is not tyrannical, such as was the original motivating factors and circumstances of the founding of the United States of America in 1776. After a period of time though, this newly-formed government of freedom eventually becomes another despotic controlling oligarchy itself, just like the one the people fled a few generations earlier, though now the current system cleverly masquerades as the benevolent democratic republic that it once was, yet is no longer. What happens next in this repeated cycle, is that this fallen government is itself eventually revolted against, just like the one before it, because of its insidious infecting corruption, and then another new government of personal liberty is again re-established to yet again secure the much treasured, but repeatedly lost, individual freedom. The next question is, what can be done to prevent this deadly cycle from perpetually repeating and how can government, with its complicit corporate and agency-controlled media, be replaced with one that is, once again, "of the people, by the people, and for the people"? Naïve President Kennedy might have thought that the original Apollo missions were "for the people", but the manner in which this operation was carried out was neither "of the people" nor "by the majority of people".

In order to appreciate the full absurdity of this lie, it bears repeating here, that what both the United States government and NASA claimed in the 1960s: On the very first attempt, and all with one-millionth the computing power of a cell phone, they had been able to send astronauts to orbit and land on the surface of the Moon, a distance that is *one thousand times* farther than they can achieve with human spaceflight today. When you finally realize the complete absurdity of this technological claim, and therefore the *genuineness* of this perpetrated Moon landing fraud, then it is far from a frivolous matter, as some might mistakenly believe, to want to bring this example of blatant, out of control government lying – specifically one that stole the modern-day equivalent of two hundred billion dollars from the American people in the process, to the attention of the overly trusting people under their care, before they are further taken advantage of by these heartless overlords.

Even if you are not yet at full acceptance of this faking of the Moon missions, if it publicly came to light that the much beloved concept of the Apollo missions was indeed a 1960s government agencies and media deception that has been maintained to this day by interested parties embedded within various groups, it will mean the end of NASA, and likely the present form of government, and this is precisely the reason why these dark forces fight so feverishly against the exposing of the Moon landing lie. Should that truth come out, then it will bring about the full exposure of all those currently within the governmental, media and other organizations still maintaining this particular lie. A long overdue government and media reformation will then indeed occur, simply out of the public's belated recognition that it is absolutely necessary for their country's good health, and the ultimate survival of governance "of the people, by the people, and for the people."

Knowing all of this is exactly why I am so passionate about this topic. While lying about going to the Moon when they failed in their ability to do so, might seem to be just one more government deception put on top of the pile of the many lies already uttered and perpetrated by our successive agencies and governments (whether Republican or Democrat), yet in this particular case, it is so symbolic of their complete lack of integrity, arrogance, and dangerously brazen attitude toward the people under their care, unless this immoral systematic behavior is immediately addressed and stopped, the life and honor of the country, the Declaration of Independence, and the people themselves, will be destroyed beyond repair.

Therefore, seeing, recognizing, acknowledging, and proclaiming this fraud is not only essential for America's survival, it is the very tool through which the country, and likely the world, can be healed and rebuilt. To do so though, will call for the utmost candor, humility, and willingness to acknowledge personal failure on the part of every member of society, as the complacency of us, the citizenry, is just as much the cause of this great systemic evil which has developed as are the perpetrators of this deceit.

The average American watches thirty-six hours of television programming or streaming a week. That's nearly as many hours as they spend at work each week. They then spend an additional twenty hours per week watching videos or surfing the internet.[2] What time is then left over for making a difference in the world? None whatsoever. This is precisely why a corrupt government likes their citizens perpetually hypnotized through television, the very vehicle through which the Moon landing deception was perpetrated on them.

This hypnotic state that most of the world is in is *not* accidental. It has been *deliberately* instituted into the culture by the corrupt people at the very top, who own and control all of this mesmerizing media, in order to keep the citizenry, which vastly outnumbers them, from becoming aware of the criminal acts being perpetually committed against them by these same overlords, so that they will not rise up and rebel against them, thusly keeping these despotic entities in indefinite financial and governmental power.

Please watch the short clip at **Sibrel.com** *Moon* Man link #3 to see the monstrous manner in which direct and subliminal hypnotizing is literally taking place every day on these entrancing screens, which are controlled by the powers who are trying to own *you.*

It is hard to fully realize that deliberate federal government brainwashing through television was going on long ago. This was precisely the time at which the supposed Moon landings took place and were screened through the medium of television, which is now far more widely available to all than it was then. Just like the blatant subliminal messages, which you will have eye-witnessed in the above clip, those telling you to submit to the obviously corrupt federal government, are highly illegal according to their own federal laws, so is it highly illegal to have embezzled the equivalent of two hundred billion dollars to fake the Moon missions. However, the laws banning such grievous crimes against the people of this nation in no way prevented the overlords from doing it anyway, as they control the courts and the legislature.

As the "magic eye" technology hidden image showcases, it makes you wonder how many newer and more technologically advanced subliminal messages could be on our many screens today. Think about the messages you are repeatedly being told on television. Generally, the exact opposite is the truth. That is what a lie is. If they are willing to lie on every television station in the world, in every newspaper in the world, and in every encyclopedia and scientific journal in the world about their historic fake Moon landings, fifty years ago when they had less control over the media than they do today, then just think about what numerous horrific lies you are being told right now.

Although I have not watched regular television myself for nearly twenty years, I did have the occasion to see it recently while in the waiting room of a local business. The national morning "news" program was ninety-five percent filled with celebrity pop-culture stories about "indulging yourself" and "caffeine is good for you" (so that you will work harder in their businesses). This is exactly what the subliminal message told us to do fifty years ago. "Indulge yourself" means "consume", that is, to consume the products of the major complicit and corrupt corporations. This makes perfect sense, as the federal government and their billion-dollar corporate bedfellows never refer to us as "people" or "Americans" or even "citizens", instead they repeatedly call us by the belittling name "consumers".

When I saw the commercials during this news program, half of them were promoting their other hypnotic television programs, a surprisingly large number of which glorified the federal government! Programs dramatizing the heroism of the FBI, CIA, FEMA and war, fill each evening's schedule. This also is exactly what the subliminal message told us to do fifty years ago in the foregoing video! It said, *"Trust the (lying) government"*. This is *exactly* the intent of these programs, to condition the viewer into trusting a federal government that is really secretly corrupt beyond measure, dramatizations specifically created to disguise this fact, along with annual programs about the fraudulent lunar landings, in order to keep the old lie alive, and the truth about it suppressed, because its revealing would be the downfall of their corruptive system.

Spending *ninety-five percent* of our waking hours in "entertainment media" (television, smartphones, tablets, and computers) is also unnatural and emotionally destructive. Proof of this is the fact that for more than a century scientists were utterly and wrongly convinced that the highly intelligent praying mantis insect was totally cannibalistic. The reason for this enduring but false belief was that the creatures studied were confined in small laboratory enclosures, as this was the most convenient method for the scientists, who then drew up their dramatically inaccurate conclusions from that study. (Sounds like the Moon landings.) Finally one researcher made a breakthrough regarding this highly publicized wrong belief. Through studying the mantis in its natural environment outside, it was revealed that the unnaturally confined and isolated laboratory conditions in which they had previously been kept had created high stress factors that induced the observed totally cannibalistic behavior.[3]

In the same way, those who continually give ninety-five percent of their waking consciousness to a simulated world instead of the real one, are voluntarily confining and isolating their own minds. It is this precise condition, first induced by television and now by other screens and devices, that not only enabled the mistaken belief in the two-dimensional falsehood of men walking on the Moon to gain credence, just like it did with the intelligent praying mantis, it turns humanity into cannibalistic self-seeking creatures, because rather than interacting with real people and real circumstances, most of our interaction becomes solely within ourselves, within our own minds, and that condition can pervasively deform the human mind into developing the inability to perceive truth.

I live near a large city park with a manmade lake. Most people who congregate there travel some distance to enjoy its nature and beauty. The other day when I was there, I saw a family of four walking around the lake together; husband, wife, teenage son and daughter. All of them had their faces in their smartphones as they walked, rather than enjoying each other's company and the beauty of the park, despite the fact that they had traveled some distance and made some effort to get there. For some strange reason we think that this is normal. Americans are becoming sleepwalking sheep who are being blindly led to the slaughter. By the time they lift their hypnotized eyes off of their screens, they will be looking up at the physicians surrounding their deathbeds.

Steve Jobs, the genius and well-meaning founder of Apple computers, iPods, iPhones, and iPad tablets, knew of this trap very well, as he forbade his own children from owning them.

The obstacle to the necessary redemption of America is, fortunately, a simple one, that of recanting the pride in the false Apollo Moon landings. The more that this lie is naïvely defended, the more support, devotion, and power is given to those corrupt entities within the government who perpetrate these lies, as well as emboldening them to carry out more of their unseen evil plans against us in the near future, which we ourselves are financing with our taxed hard labor!

Like a disciplined athlete refusing sugary sweets, the citizen addicted to the Moon landing candy, which was fed to them since birth from their beloved and respected leaders, must be willfully laid down and the sobering painful truth must be openly welcomed, otherwise America will *never* attain its cure. If this is not done, then there is no hope whatsoever for their or their country's recovery. Sometimes cutting off a diseased limb is necessary to save the body. If such a truth-based operation is not done, or postponed, then the gangrene of evil will grow and grow to such a degree that the entire nation-body will be infected so severely that it will die from its own lethal bad habits, like a smoker who knows that they should quit after their lung cancer operation but who continues smoking through their tracheotomy anyway.

I am grieved that I have to paint such a dark picture, yet unless

I do so, the cancer that is necessary to be seen and removed, in order to proceed to our personal and nation's health, will never occur. There is hope though, that there are those out there in the federal government who love truth and honor more than life itself, just as our Founding Fathers and Mothers did, who risked their entire lives and fortunes for their noble dream of establishing a country wherein the individual, not the governing overlords, holds the supremacy over their own life and freedom. We are all going to die anyway, so why not take an important stand for justice and truth, even at the cost of life?

So many of us fear when we see a police officer, rather than welcoming them as our beloved brother or sister, because we know that they are an agent of this runaway, power hungry, fine-collecting, harsh, and cruel governmental system, that fakes Moon landings, kills presidents, and taxes the middle class at three times a higher percentage than the wealthy. It was Thomas Jefferson who said, "When the people fear the government, there is tyranny. When the government fears the people, there is liberty," and which of the two systems do we have at this hour? The answer is very clear.

The United States government is in *no way whatsoever* a government "of the people, by the people, and for the people". It is a corporate and CIA oligarchy disguised as such, whose sleepwalking citizens defend the very crimes perpetrated against them to their own demise, such as the fraudulent Moon landings.

Wake up people! Technology does not go backwards! As I have already stated, if the federal government could put a man on the Moon on the very first attempt, then there would be bases on the moon by now. The longer the majority of Americans are hypnotized about this (and other crimes against them by the federal government) the more hopeless the situation becomes.

You know now why the Moon Man is so passionate about this topic of the Moon landing deception, because it so symbolically represents the deplorable state of the United States federal government, which so desperately needs to be completely overhauled.

"All truth passes through three stages...
First, it is ridiculed...
Then, it is violently opposed...
Finally, it is accepted as self-evident."

– *Arthur Schopenhauer*

Chapter Two
How All This Began

H aving presented my overview of the big picture, I will continue the chronological story of my involvement with this
matter from where we left off, back in 1989, when I was
24 and working as a filmmaker for the producer of the program
on which NASA contractor and science writer Bill Kaysing had
espoused the Moon landing fraud – and opened my eyes to this
topic some ten years previously. As a result of that amazing providence, my producer facilitated a connection to Bill, with whom
I then started a lifelong friendship, first over the telephone, and
then later in person.

It was Bill Kaysing who first suggested that I should make
a documentary film questioning the authenticity of the alleged
Moon landings. As an established filmmaker, the idea seemed logical to me, so I studied the subject, pretty much full time, for six
months. I discovered that it was the Soviet Union, not the United
States, that put the first satellite into space, the first animal in
space, the first man in space, the first woman in space and the
first man to orbit the Earth, plus the first spacewalk and the first
of two spacecraft orbiting simultaneously. At that time the Soviets
had spent five times more man hours in space than that of the
United States. As the Russians were the repeated "boogiemen"
used to justify the USA spending more on military hardware than
all of the other leading countries of the world combined (even
though Russia and China have no desire whatsoever to invade
America), the idea of this supposed "enemy" beating the United
States in a field of a new technological frontier, pierced the pride
of the leaders of the self-proclaimed "greatest nation on Earth".

Thusly, the "Space Race" had begun in 1957 with the advent of the first orbiting satellite, the Soviet Union's Sputnik. By 1961, when John F. Kennedy inherited this race along with his presidency, these two superpowers were ready to send men into space, or so they thought. In response to the Soviet's first spaceflight of cosmonaut Yuri Gagarin on April 12, 1961, the United States launched its first astronaut, Alan Shepard, into space on May 7, 1961. Shortly thereafter on May 25, Kennedy naïvely decided to boldly proclaim, "We will put a man on the Moon by the end of the decade." Seeing how Alan Shepard had only flown a fifteen-minute parabolic orbit of just over *three hundred miles* with a maximum altitude of 116 miles compared to Gagarin (who was in space for one hour forty-eight minutes, flying a complete twenty-five thousand mile orbit of the Earth at a maximum altitude of 203 miles) that was incredibly optimistic. American astronauts did not achieve a full orbit of Earth until 1962, by which time the end of the decade was only eight and a half years into the future. Yet back in 1961, if manned rockets could already reach "outer space" (albeit this was merely one to two hundred miles above the Earth) and even though the Moon's average orbit is about two hundred and thirty-eight thousand miles away, this goal seemed at least possible. Little did President Kennedy know that landing a man on the Moon and returning him safely to Earth would soon thereafter prove to be a scientific impossibility, as it is even to this day with conventional technology, otherwise Moon bases would exist today. Regrettably, (as he would later recognize) with this premature and naïve technological boast about distant future equipment that had yet to be invented, successfully developed and tested, the new well-meaning president had put the nation's prideful reputation on the line in full view of the world.

King Solomon said, "Pride comes before a fall," and a very great fall it would be. People and nations are forever committing errors due to pride. In my opinion pride is the greatest obstacle to facing facts. Thusly, to make up for Kennedy's premature boast made on the world stage, which could not be fulfilled, a *fictional* Moon landing was created in place of reality. When I discovered these three truths that:

- Despite their technical supremacy in space the Soviets never sent a man to the Moon, not even *once* in the last fifty years.
- James Webb, the second administrator of NASA, served from February 14, 1961 through to October 7, 1968. Having overseen all the Mercury and Gemini crewed flights, he resigned just ten weeks before the lunar orbiting Apollo 8 mission was scheduled for launch.[4]
- Two of the three US astronauts of the first supposed lunar landing rarely gave public interviews about the alleged "greatest achievement of mankind".

Taken together with my own realization that the stark lighting anomalies in the photographs which were allegedly taken on the Moon (which as an experienced filmmaker I recognized as television studio electrical lighting instead of the claimed sunlight), I eventually came to the sobering conclusion that there was *at least* a one-in-four chance that the acclaimed Moon missions were in fact a dark government deception, just as Bill Kaysing so confidently asserted from his own first-hand eyewitness experience.

Just as if the police were to inform me that one of my four neighbors might be an serial killer on the loose, I found that a one-in-four chance that the proclaimed "greatest achievement of mankind," might instead be a manipulative CIA deception, to be quite an alarming percentage, yet that was the conclusion of my six months of preliminary study. Following this initial research, when Bill Kaysing suggested that I should produce a documentary on this subject, I actually became fearful at the prospect. I knew, since my youth, that I had always been attracted to puzzles. I even drew complicated mazes as a child for friends to solve that even adults found perplexing. I also realized that I possessed a somewhat relentless nature, in that I had the drive to succeed at a task, no matter how difficult, once I had begun it. Knowing these two things about myself, I thought that if anyone could get to the bottom of this mystery, I could. Yet, I asked myself, "Do I really want to investigate such a dark matter? Because if they *really* falsified the Moon landing events, and I started overturning rocks that the CIA, NASA and other agencies want to remain undisturbed, then I could be risking my life in the process."

Thusly, I was quite fearful of seriously investigating the supposed Moon landings. I said to myself, "Why should I risk my life for someone else's folly? I plan to get married and have children someday." Therefore I initially turned down this documentary film project because of this very real, potentially life-threatening danger.

Despite that, Bill and I continued to talk several times a year, as he well understood my reluctance. Bill became my adopted grandfather, as both my natural ones had died before I was born. I still continued to quietly investigate the subject and would regularly call him with questions about the Apollo program.

Then in June 1989 a life-changing event happened, again through one of my film clients. I was working for a well-known Christian musician at the time, whose wife proposed an interesting trade. She knew that I had written several unproduced screenplays, which I hoped someday would be made into feature films either by myself or sold and directed by others. She also knew a famous producer in Hollywood and said that she would personally deliver one of my screenplays to him if I would do her a favor. "What favor?" I asked. "Read the Bible," she said.

"Humm... I contemplated, "Read the Bible for one chance in a lifetime to advance my film career? Sure!" She suggested I use a "One Year Bible" (this has the entire contents divided into 365 daily sections). I started reading the Bible on June 5, 1989, the same day that a brave man stood in front of a tank in China's Tiananmen Square to protect his countrymen from its onslaught, and to protest his own government's rampant tyranny. Over the next couple of years I kept up the habit of reading my Bible every day until I had read it all the way through twice, and then an event involving Jim Irwin occurred.

Bill Kaysing told me that on August 5, 1991, Apollo 15 astronaut James Irwin had tracked Bill down and called him to arrange a private conversation with Kaysing over the telephone. After his

1971 Apollo 15 mission, Irwin had become a devout "Born again Christian", holding creationist beliefs and he had spent from 1973 through to the late 1980s searching for Noah's Ark on Mount Ararat. Bill related to me how Irwin said that he had seen his July 5, 1981 interview with Oprah Winfrey in Baltimore, Maryland, when Bill was spearheading the cause for the disclosure of the truth about the Moon landings. Irwin confided that he needed to tell Bill something very important about the Apollo missions. Colonel Irwin said that he was concerned for his safety if he was discovered talking about the matter with Bill, and asked that Kaysing give him a call back in three days time, using a telephone number that was secure in Irwin's opinion.

On August 8, 1991, the very day that Apollo fraud investigator Bill Kaysing and Apollo 15 astronaut James Irwin were supposed to have a "very important conversation about the Moon missions", and just prior to the scheduled telephone call, Colonel James Irwin suffered a fatal heart attack.

I realized this occurring as it did, three days after telling Bill that he had something very important to say about the Apollo program and stressing that he was concerned for his safety – the odds of James Irwin's death being a random fatal happenstance was extremely unlikely. As it took place on the very same day that the astronaut was scheduled to talk to the leading Moon landing fraud investigator, this "heart attack" should not be considered a coincidence. As you can understand, coming to these conclusions gave me another severe bout of apprehension about looking ever more deeply into this matter.

I continued on with my professional work and my Bible readings for another three years, although unfortunately for my screenwriting career, the Hollywood film producer died before he received my script. Fortunately for my Moon landing documentary this was an important turning point in both my spiritual life as well as in the life of A Funny Thing Happened on the Way to the Moon. (Hereinafter abbreviated to A Funny Thing Happened...)

I had now begun to realize a few things. First of all, the rather obvious fact that like everyone else I'm mortal and I am going to die whether or not I make the documentary about the fraud. Secondly, I realized that there is good and evil, and that if the Moon landings were indeed falsified, then as far as I was concerned, that was definitely wrong. I also realized that due to the great international historical significance of the supposed event, faked lunar missions were an even more profound event than if they had actually gone to the Moon. In my opinion, humankind was being robbed of a precious humbling lesson, in that recognizing the truth about the falsification of the Apollo project, would inevitably bring a great betterment to the individual, the nation, and the world at large. It was at that point I decided that if I was going to die, I might as well die for a just cause. Five years after I had initially turned down the project, I changed my mind. I immediately called up Bill and told him so. He was delighted. Bill's book called *We Never Went to the Moon* (first published in 1975) had naturally been my primary research material. Then in 1992, Ralph René, a high IQ Mensa member, published *NASA Mooned America* which I also read. I then watched any and every film on the subject of a potential Moon mission fraud (which were mostly unrefined home movies), as well as studying all of the Apollo photographs and footage which I could obtain.

From 1994 to 1996 I researched NASA's Apollo program. I sold off some of the assets of my television production company to finance my research during the week, which consumed a lot of unpaid time. I also landed a part-time weekend job at an NBC affiliate working in the news department as a videotape editor, cameraman, and as a reporter, thanks to my varied technical and theatrical experience. When two years later the news director found out that I was preparing a story about the Moon landing fraud for submission and had used my media credentials from the station to get access to question Neil Armstrong on the subject, he fired me for "putting the network in a bad light." Oddly enough, in the 1978 film *Capricorn One*, about a fake *Mars* landing, the main character, played by Elliott Gould, also worked at an NBC affiliate as a reporter and likewise was fired for working on such a "preposterous" story, that also ended up being true.

I could now devote all of my attention to the project, and by the end of 1996 I started to write the narration for my film *A Funny Thing Happened...* This had been **an alternative title** to Ralph René's book that I liked so much that I adopted it for my film. By 1998 I had edited together the first ten minutes or so of the movie. Most of the seven years which it took to make the film were spent meticulously researching the subject so that I would be certain of my assertions. I told NASA's media department that I was making a documentary about the Moon landings, which was true, intentionally neglecting to tell them that I was questioning the missions' authenticity in the process, for fear of losing their cooperation in sending me the film footage and photographs necessary for my research and insertion into the film.

In 1998, four years into the seven-year project, I met a highly successful millionaire who had made his fortune in the technology sector and who was a board member of an aerospace company building rockets for NASA. His IQ was up there with Einstein's and he knew, from an engineering standpoint, that the massive Saturn V rocket (the one used in the supposed attempts to go to the Moon) did not have enough fuel and power to leave Earth orbit, that the Apollo onboard guidance computer (AGC) used to interface with the ground-based mainframes (just one-millionth as fast as a modern cell phone) did not have the capability to convert the data for the thousands of miles per hour trajectories in real time. It is worth recalling that the **AGC had just 4KB** of memory, and the Lunar Module (the flimsy craft that supposedly landed on the lunar surface) did not have enough battery power to run the air conditioning system for three days against the lunar outside temperatures of some 250° Fahrenheit (121° C/394.15K). Neither did it have any ability to shield against solar radiation, let alone an unpredictable Solar Particle Event. This astute millionaire knew more than I did that the alleged Moon missions were really a clever and outrageous government deception. When I told him of my "one-in-four chance" estimation of the probability of Moon landing fakery, he said, "No Bart. A 100% chance."

It was this wealthy person who largely financed my documen-

tary and became its executive producer. Because of his high-ranking status with a NASA contractor and within the technology
sector, he wishes to continue to remain anonymous. He financed
my film out of his patriotism for our country's Founding Fathers
and because of his disgust of such blatant and arrogant high-level
governmental fraud.

While I already owned professional camera and editing equipment as a filmmaker, funds from this individual allowed me to
decline other projects and devote myself full-time to making the
documentary. We also purchased expensive original documentation from some of the estates of the widows of former Apollo
astronauts as part of our extensive research. Funds were also used
to buy the rights to the music and archive footage that was used
in the film. Another financier was an ex-military pilot who also
had first hand knowledge of the deception just as Bill Kaysing did.

Both of these remarkable people considered it their patriotic
duty to expose this fraud and that is why they financed my two
films on the subject. (Right now as I write this, there are about one
hundred thousand individual whistleblower complaints of fraud
against the Pentagon that are not being investigated). While both
of these men were one hundred percent certain that the Moon
landings were staged and pre-created, at this point in the timeline
of my story I was yet to be fully convinced myself. I needed concrete proof. I suppose I still hoped, for humanity's sake, that we
had not stooped so low as to do such a deplorable thing. When
you really think about it, falsifying the Apollo Moon landings was
an incredibly despicable act to perpetrate upon the world.

"In an age of universal deceit,
telling the truth is a revolutionary act."
"Whoever controls the past, controls the future."

– *George Orwell*

Chapter Three
The Day My Life Changed Forever

Please watch this seventeen-minute video of my quick summary of what we are about to discuss in this chapter, **Sibrel.com** *Moon Man* link **#4**.

By the summer of 1999, I was well into the editing of the documentary *A Funny Thing Happened...* through which I intended to submit for public review the very real possibility that the nation's proud Moon landing events were indeed a criminal deception. One of the reasons that the documentary took the seven years to produce, aside from the tremendous amount of research, was the film editing process. Eight years earlier in 1991 when I was twenty six, I had won three separate awards from the American Motion Picture Society in the same film festival for best editing, best cinematography, and top ten director. In fact, the longtime director of the film society said, "I was making movies when this competition started way back in 1930. I do not recall anyone ever entering three motion pictures and winning a top award on all three. But you have!"

I won these unprecedented three awards simultaneously by being meticulous. I suppose you could say that I am a perfectionist. I always strive to make every television commercial or music video which I produce as good as humanly possible. The same was true of this documentary questioning the authenticity of the Moon missions. As such, I spent about four thousand hours editing the forty-seven minute film. That is about forty hours a week for two years.

In the process of this, I felt that it would be dramatic to show the launch of the first rocket allegedly going to the Moon in real

time, from about one minute before the launch to about a half
a minute afterwards, or a minute and a half straight through
without any editing. Unfortunately, all of the footage that I had
obtained from NASA was pre-edited, and of these many repetitious pre-edited reels, none of them showed the launch of the
supposed maiden voyage to the Moon without skipping ahead in
the countdown. I therefore called my contact at NASA's media
department and asked him for this footage, informing him that it
was essential for the completion of my film. Instead, I received a
reel of footage completely unrelated to my request. I called again,
explaining once more, as precisely as I could, that I wanted the
rocket countdown of Apollo 11, unedited, in either film or videotape. I was then sent the wrong reel a second time. I telephoned
NASA a third time, again stressing that I could not finish my film
without this footage, and reiterated, in very simple terms, that I
wanted the complete unedited countdown of Apollo 11, in either
videotape or film. I then received a completely unrelated reel for
the third time.

Perhaps I should not have said that without this footage I could
not finish my film, as when I telephoned NASA the fourth time,
something even more unusual happened. On a previous occasion
this government agency had told me that they were so underfund-
ed they inventoried individual paperclips and had only recently
upgraded to a broadcast videotape standard that had been around
for more than ten years (which I had already owned for sometime
in my small television production company). Now, suddenly they
volunteered to pay for my postage of all future reels of footage, although this would be much slower than Federal Express, which I
had previously used and paid for myself. When I said "no" to their
generous offer, they insisted that future shipments of footage to
me, which I needed to complete my documentary, would be transported in their stipulated slower manner, with an estimated deliv-
ery time of six weeks, instead of the twenty-four hours to which I
had been accustomed.

At this unusual development, I became alarmed. It appeared
to me that NASA was intentionally trying to stall my project. De-

ductive logic then asked, "Why would they do this?" to which I replied, "Because they know what I am up to." Oops! As I had only thought that there was a one-in-four chance that the lunar landings were fraudulent, though this percentage was still too high for my comfort, I really had not taken any precautions as to the security and secrecy of my project. For many years I had openly talked about my upcoming documentary about the fraud over the telephone with my anonymous benefactor, with Bill Kaysing and with numerous other people involved in the project, including confidential sources who were astronauts or their immediate family members.

A few years ago William Binney, who served for thirty-two years as a high-ranking intelligence officer with the National Security Agency (NSA), an offshoot of the Central Intelligence Agency (CIA), became a "whistleblower" (one who sounds the alarm of rampant government corruption, like Bill Kaysing and myself) and publicly confessed that the NSA and CIA regularly listen to the telephone conversations of US Presidents, Supreme Court Justices, and members of the Congress and Senate, for the express purpose of collecting "dirt" on them, so that they can be blackmailed into unethical decision making by these corrupt, unelected rogue intelligence agencies, whose native language, as spies, is lies. So reliable and undeniably true was Binney's confession of this rampant corruption, which became part of the public record, that all of it eventually had to be acknowledged by the mainstream media (although as a minor side note). It was only the alternative media (like myself) who treated Mr. Binney's disclosure with the supreme importance it deserved. The sad fact is, there was never any investigation whatsoever into this blatant violation of privacy and extortion laws perpetrated by the Federal Government on its own high-ranking citizens, and there were never any congressional hearings into what were acknowledged to be completely true and obvious felonies committed by the Federal Government against its own people. Absolutely unbelievable!

How can this be? How can it be that it is publicly acknowledged, and never contested, that the NSA and the CIA spy on the private conversations of all United States Presidents, Supreme Court justices, and members of the Congress and Senate, for the purpose of blackmailing them into making unethical executive, legislative, and judicial decisions, yet no one does anything about it? After this came to light, do you still doubt that the supposed Moon landings could have been falsified?

Thusly, if these Apollo missions were indeed a fraud, and its exposure might lead to the dismantling of such corrupt agencies because of public outrage, then I suspect that these same agencies would indeed keep up with the project of a documentary being made to expose this fraud. This was the reason, I realized, that NASA was trying to stall my project. If the government really had successfully landed on the Moon, I would just be a sadly mistaken individual and my project would be unworthy of any attention. Knowing that I had lost NASA's cooperation with my project, I therefore took up a search which I had abandoned months earlier because all of the footage that I had gone through so far was very limited, repetitious, and even though I had specifically and repeatedly asked NASA for *un-edited* footage, as already stated, all that I was sent over and over again, was the same limited *pre-edited* footage generally filled with propagandized voiceovers of the glory of the supposed missions. I then proceeded to double-check all the reels which I had already received, in the hopes of my finding the un-edited countdown of the first Apollo launch.

My thinking was this: If they faked the Moon landings, they were more likely to have made a mistake the *first* time that they had faked it, due to their inexperience in doing so. Thusly, I had exclusively asked NASA for photographs and footage from just the first mission, Apollo 11. In fact, I told NASA that because I was a very thorough filmmaker, to please send me *every* single photograph and reel of footage from the first Moon mission. To my incredible surprise, there were actually very few pictures of the two acclaimed astronauts allegedly standing on the Moon, very few, only about two dozen. Considering that it was supposed to be the "greatest event in human history", this lack of record seems very odd. In fact, I could not find a *single* still photograph of the most famous man in the world at the time, Neil Armstrong, claiming to be standing on the lunar surface. When I went in person to the NASA archives in search of such an image, to all of the librarians' extraordinary astonishment, there were no still pictures of Neil Armstrong standing on the surface of the Moon. Not a single one. It looked as if Neil Armstrong did not want a permanent historical record of his participation in such a great fraud, which might one day be exposed, so it really does appear that he refused to be photographed doing it. (The grainy television images, wherein the astronauts' faces were hidden by reflective visors, were likely to have been stand-ins. My later research confirmed this probability.)

NASA's excuse for there not being any photographs of Neil Armstrong on the lunar surface is that he had their one and only camera mounted to his chest, and therefore only Aldrin appears in the pictures, and he was the only astronaut of the three assigned to the first mission who would later give regular interviews. Don't you think that if you were truly at a location where there is no air pressure, a two hundred and fifty degree temperature difference between light and shadowed areas, along with vast amounts of solar and cosmic radiation and exposure to micrometeorites, that you might want to have more than one camera as a backup, just to be sure to have a record of the greatest event in human history? What if one of them had dropped the one and only camera? What if the aforementioned hazards ruined the camera's mechanics and subsequently there was no photographic record at all of such an historic event? Why not improve the odds by giving them *each* a camera? The only pictures allegedly of Neil Armstrong on the lunar surface were taken by a time-lapse **motion picture** camera mounted on the side of the lunar module (LM), one distant side view image, and one of his tiny reflection in Aldrin's visor, none of which show his face or name insignia. Some pictures from the mission even mistakenly labeled Aldrin as Armstrong, in a desperate attempt to cover up this obvious discrepancy, and the likely insistence from Armstrong that he not be photographed during this deception.

Quite surprising, isn't it? Even the NASA librarians at their own archives were highly perplexed when my investigation brought this to their attention. The alleged greatest achievement of mankind, the first man on the Moon, and of the individual who supposedly accomplished it, there is not a *single* still picture of him doing so! Remarkable!

In order to refute this glaring oversight, and the lack of an extensive photographic record of the first astronauts claiming to be standing on the supposed lunar surface, NASA later claimed (fifty years later) that the agency had "thousands" of pictures of the Apollo missions. If you include hundreds of pictures of the astronauts training on Earth, hundreds of pictures from Earth of the rocket launches, hundreds of pictures from inside the spacecraft, and hundreds of pictures of the Earth and Moon from outer space (which were actually taken from unmanned probes or a spacecraft while only in Earth orbit), then yes, this figure might be accurate. The point is the scarcity of high quality photographs of astronauts supposedly standing on the lunar surface, especially during the first most important mission, where there are only about two dozen pictures, and as already stated, not a single one clearly showing Neil Armstrong himself as the purported "first man on the Moon". Surely if someone went on holiday, and especially if they were visiting a distant and exotic location, they would have hundreds of pictures of themselves, not a measly two dozen. In my mind the reason for this scarcity of a photographic record is simply because it is in these maiden fake pictures where there is the best opportunity to expose the fraud, so these are the very ones of which there are the fewest.

These were my thoughts as I meticulously went through the remaining tape reels that NASA had sent me, searching for any trace of an unedited Apollo 11 launch. When I finally got to the bottom of the pile and popped in the second to the last of the reels, it immediately said on the screen **Not For General Public Distribution**.

This film
of the Apollo 11 Mission
was produced
as a report film by
THE MANNED SPACECRAFT CENTER
and is not
for general public distribution

I said to myself, "This should be interesting." As usual, I hit the fast forward button, because as an editor of tens of thousands of hours of footage over the previous two decades, I had developed the ability to recognize images even when being scanned at about twenty times normal speed.

To my surprise, I kept seeing the same individual image continually, with only slight variations in movement, for ten minutes, fifteen minutes, and then for more than twenty minutes. I quickly realized that I had stumbled upon the only *un-edited* footage of the Apollo 11 mission that I had yet seen. When I popped out the reel and checked the label to see what it was called, I also realized that what the reel contained was actually very different from what the label said it contained. Apparently someone, way back in 1969, had mistakenly put the wrong label on the reel and its container, and it had therefore been placed into the material available to the public, instead of logging it into the "not for general public distribution" private library. No doubt because every media outlet had been completely satisfied with just the first reel or two of pre-edited NASA footage from the Apollo missions, always used for their repeated brief anniversary commemorations, this particular reel and its apparent mislabeling mistake, had never before been discovered. Apparently no one had ever asked for *every* single reel of footage from the *first* lunar landing mission, Apollo 11 – until I came along. (Bill Kaysing thought that a whistleblower at NASA sent the revealing footage to me intentionally.)

As I fast-forwarded through the reel's ninety minutes or so of this odd continuous footage, it was the image (as shown here) that I kept seeing for most of the duration. Imagine a television screen being mostly black, with a blue softball sized "Earth" in the middle of it, supposedly surrounded by the blackness of space, with the camera constantly being adjusted in an attempt to perfect the shot. After I popped out the reel to look at the label on it and discovered that what it described and what the reel actually contained were two very different things, I rewound it to the beginning and hit the "Play" button to watch it at normal speed. **"Hello Apollo 11. Houston** (speaking). **Goldstone** [the Californian satellite tracking station] **says that the TV** [picture] **looks great. Over."**

These were the first words that I heard over the unusual image. Next, there was a four-second pause. After this, a third party, (clandestine, so presumably the CIA) prompted the crew by saying **"Talk."** Immediately after this prompting, it was Neil Armstrong who replied on cue and said, **"OK. Roger. We're zooming** [the camera] **in on Earth."** Noteworthy was the fact that this third "confidential" party, had much clearer audio than NASA or the astronauts. This stranger's voice did not have the "radio sound" that NASA and the astronauts did. It was as if this undisclosed man was at the same location where the videotape was secretly being recorded.

When watching this footage for the very first time, I did not fully realize that the astronauts, who were claiming to be halfway to the Moon, were in reality still in Earth orbit, from which they never left until they splashed down in the ocean eight days later. The reason why the CIA was covertly prompting Armstrong to speak, only *after* four seconds had elapsed, was to create the illusion of Armstrong being a great distance from the Earth ("130,000 miles out" as he claimed), when he was really orbiting the Earth at a nearby distance of about 250 miles. Again, the Apollo 11 crew was **supposed to be** halfway to the Moon, therefore there was a radio transmission time delay to be falsified. If Armstrong had answered NASA immediately, it would have given away the fact that he was only about two hundred and fifty miles above the Earth, rather than the one hundred and thirty thousand miles that was falsely claimed. The actual time delay for the distance of 130,000 miles was of 1.5 seconds there and back. (Even from the Moon's surface at the time of Apollo 11, the time lag is 2.7 seconds there and back, at most). Furthermore, the ninety-minute length of this tape is equivalent to one spacecraft Earth Orbit, as near as you can get without getting pulled back into the atmosphere. So I maintain that the Apollo 11 crew never left low-Earth orbit, they stayed at an altitude of about two hundred fifty miles, or where the International Space Station orbits, and that is still the limit of travel for all astronauts today.

Another interesting thing about this amazing and condemning footage is that it was the only fake photography of the mission actually filmed by the astronauts themselves. Although they told the television audience that their camera's lens was right up against the glass of the circular window which faced the Earth (as it would have to be if they were really filming the Earth outside of

the spacecraft's window from some great distance away from it),
the camera was *in reality* at the *back* of the spacecraft, *several feet
away from the window.* The Apollo 11 crew was secretly instructed
to block out the sunlight from entering the spacecraft through the
other windows and to turn off all the lights, so that the interior
of the spacecraft would be dark, and that the walls of the spacecraft around the circular window would not be revealed. They talk
about all of this clandestine preparation in this un-edited reel,
having been told that these private conversations of theirs about
their deception would be edited out before it was broadcast to
the public. This pre-editing of a supposedly live broadcast, they
also openly talk about in this un-edited, raw footage, referring to
the deceptive "live" segment that was really intended for playback
after it had been edited to appear genuine. All of this is precisely
why the first frame of this one-of-a-kind footage was labeled, "**Not
For General Public Distribution**".

As the astronauts were really in low-Earth orbit while they
falsely claimed to be "halfway to the Moon", the window they
claimed to be filming through was actually filled with the bright
light of earthshine reflecting off the Earth just beneath them. The
astronauts placed a transparent color photograph (transparency)
of the circular Earth, some twelve inches so in width, in front of
the circular window. This transparent photo was perfectly backlit
by the reflecting earthshine, like a color x-ray on top of a project-
ing light box. The Apollo 11 crew then very carefully inserted a
black crescent shaped piece of material on top of their one-foot
transparency of the Earth to make it look like it was the dividing
"terminator line" between night and day. With the camera at the
back of the spacecraft filming this, and with the interior of the
spacecraft completely dark, it looked as if the Earth was floating
in space at some great distance away, when it was *really* just a
transparency of the circular Earth in front of the brightly backlit
circular window from Earth orbit! Ingenious!

It was a very convincing illusion, intended to trick the television audience into believing that the Apollo spacecraft, at that
point in the mission, was halfway to the Moon, when in reality

they were still in low-Earth orbit. Had I not received this very revealing unedited behind-the-scenes footage, of which only about one minute was ever broadcast to the public, I doubt if I would have figured out this clever deception. In fact, I originally thought that instead of a backlit image of the circular Earth placed on top of the window, I was seeing a portion of the Earth outside of the circular window from Earth orbit, which then formed the same illusion, and I had the narrator of my film say so.

After my film was released, a fellow filmmaker pointed out this misunderstanding to me. (Interestingly and supporting the whistle-blowing theory suggested by Bill Kaysing, this same filmmaker had also received this footage within a bundle of material he had requested from NASA at about the same time as I did. Some detractors of my film tried to use my initial interpretation as proof that I was wrong in general. Yet the fact remains, either way, what we are seeing is definitely a forgery using an image of the Earth, rather than the *real* Earth surrounded by the blackness of space, proving beyond a doubt that Apollo 11 never left low-Earth orbit, and thusly the astronauts could have never reached the Moon, let alone walked on its surface. As all of the following Apollo missions had identical Earth-orbit limited equipment, it means that the United States never put a man on the Moon, not even once.

Some diehard fans of the alleged missions, who have seen *A Funny Thing Happened...* and this revealing footage contained therein, have even publicly admitted that this NASA forgery of the "Earth floating in space" is indeed a fake. They justify its existence by claiming that "the astronauts were just rehearsing". I am so glad that they said this. First of all, the biggest fans of the alleged Moon missions have now publicly acknowledged that at least *part* of the Apollo 11 photography of the Moon mission presented as the Apollo record is indeed fake. Significantly, this exact footage, which NASA fans now openly acknowledge is a forgery, is the very same footage that is used in all of the NASA Apollo documentaries in which they claim this very same false footage is genuine! The reality is, if they really had gone to the

Moon, why would *any* of the photography need to be faked?

Secondly, if they were *really* halfway to the Moon and the Earth was *really* floating in space just outside the window, then why would the crew bother bringing a photograph of the Earth along with them to create this illusion? Thirdly, if the crew was "rehearsing", then why not rehearse with the real Earth floating in space outside the window? There would be no need to rehearse with an elaborate, time-consuming, falsification of the Earth in space. They would just rehearse with the real Earth outside of the window and rightly put the camera lens up against the glass of the window, instead of lying about having the camera lens up against the glass window, when it was really at the back of the spacecraft in order to create this falsification!

Immediately after my documentary was released other diehard NASA fans, for whom the alleged Moon landings are sacrosanct (and this is precisely why they cannot see so many obvious truthful flaws), intentionally lied about this newly discovered revealing footage, just as their idolized astronauts did. They said that this highly condemning fraudulent footage, "is meaningless as it has been publicly available for years." Really? Is this why it says "Not for General Public Distribution" at the very beginning of the reel? These deniers of truth (who I guess because of pride will not admit that they are wrong about their beloved Moon missions), even showed part of this false footage in a NASA compilation of their own, yet only *after* my film came out. This is additional proof that the footage was not available previously as they falsely claimed. In *their* version of this condemning footage (available on DVD from Spacecraft Films), they even *intentionally edited out* the "anonymous voice" (in my opinion, a clandestine CIA agent) who after that intentional four-second delay, told Armstrong to "talk" in order to create the deceitful appearance of a radio delay, to give the false impression of being halfway to the Moon, when the crew was really still in Earth orbit.

The question is: if this newly-discovered recording of the "anonymous voice" (presumably CIA) and the intentional four-second delay is of no consequence as my critics falsely claimed

– then why was it necessary for them to edit out these highly condemning sections from their version of this footage?

When I studied this footage for the very first time, it took me a moment to figure out the deception, as I first saw the thick, battleship-like width around the inside of the circular window, which the astronauts had made up to look like the outer border of the circular Earth. Next, I saw a few "outtakes" or mistakes of theirs, such as when an astronaut's arm mistakenly moved in front of the one-foot image of the Earth, as shown below.

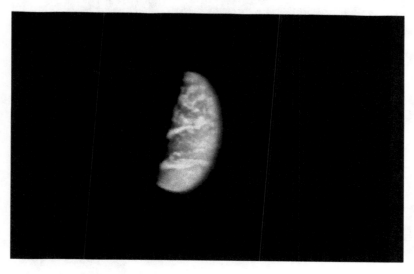

After this, I saw the real position of the camera at the *back* of the spacecraft as a work light came into view while they were taking down the photograph of the Earth in front of the circular window, with their hands visibly removing it. All of this was then followed by the lights being switched back on in the spacecraft, enabling me to see that the round shape, which was the location of the image of the Earth seen only moments earlier, was *in fact* the circular window. I then saw the very bright earthshine outside of the window, resulting from the craft being in Earth orbit, *rather than halfway to the Moon.*

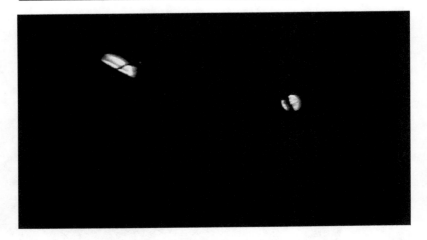

I then fully realized that the camera had actually been at the back of the spacecraft the entire time, not up against the window glass as had been falsely stated for the deceived television audience. The camera's lens would have to be up against the window if they were really halfway to the Moon and the Earth really was at some 130,000 miles distant, in order to film such a thing as their forgery suggested.

The module window that previously had the transparency of the Earth placed up against it.

As apparent as the deception seems now, when I was viewing it for the very first time and was initially figuring out what I was seeing as the reel progressed, the process of this life-changing revelation seemed slow. "That's not the window is it, that they are using to create a fake Earth? Surely not!" I said to myself. Yet, when the lights were turned back on and I saw where the camera had been located, and that the astronauts had used a photograph of the Earth as a substitute for the real thing, then I realized that they had never left Earth orbit. It then slowly began to dawn on me that the concrete proof of the fraud that I had so long desired was now in my possession. It was a sad and life-changing moment indeed. I actually wept quietly.

"Let me understand this..." I said to myself. "They are faking being halfway to the Moon. That is definitely what they are doing." I went on to say, and realized as I was saying it, "If they are faking being hallway to the Moon, then this means that they *cannot even go halfway to the Moon*... I then said to myself, "If they were incapable of leaving low-Earth orbit, they certainly could not have gone all the way to the Moon. As all the Apollo flights used the exact same equipment, if one mission's craft can't leave Earth orbit, then it means that none of them ever did so... which means that undeniably, no one has ever gone to the Moon."

I then exclaimed, "Wow!" as I quickly realized that I had proof in my meager possession of one of the greatest deceptions of the century, perhaps of all time, without taking any security precautions whatsoever! I had thought that there would never be any concrete proof of the Moon landing fraud discovered in my lifetime.

Only the previous week, when I realized that my telephone conversations must be monitored because of NASA's sudden lack of cooperation with my project, did I get the production staff to swap cell phones to a provider that scrambled (encrypted) the voice transmissions. This, as it turned out, was a big mistake, now that I look back on it, after having done more research about such things since then – as the very first flag of attention that the CIA and the NSA look for when they are scanning communications around the world, is people who scramble or encrypt their telephone conversations or emails for secrecy! Oops! (Doing so actually makes the CIA/NSA especially focus in on such communications, which then receive a higher priority of attention than previously.) Looking back on it, naïvely and optimistically thinking that I could outwit the CIA with such a simple civilian measure was a laughable mistake.

Nevertheless, the first thing I did when I discovered this condemning footage from the first mission was to call up Bill Kaysing and tell him the good news of my amazing discovery on our newly-scrambled telephones. "They *really* didn't go to the Moon!" I exclaimed to Bill, over and over again in my excitement, "They *really* didn't go!" Bill calmly replied, "Well Bart, I told you that ten years ago." I still rebutted, "Yeah, but they really didn't go!" He repeated, "Well Bart, I told you that ten years ago." I laugh now recalling this. Bill was probably laughing at that time too.

It was June 30, 1999 when all of this happened. I was still two years away from completing the film *"A Funny Thing Happened..."* I told Bill about the fact that NASA appeared to be on to our true intentions for the Apollo documentary, because they were no longer cooperating with sending me footage, and now that I had proof in my possession of the Moon landing fraud that the United States federal government and its agencies had perpetrated in 1969, I advised Bill to not sleep in the same location that he had slept in last night. The moment that I said this to him, our telephone conversation was suddenly interrupted with a loud constant screech, one so loud, that it was nearly impossible to hear or understand each other over it. I implored Bill Kaysing again not to sleep where he slept last night. After this second warning, our telephone connection was terminated and could not be re-established for nearly a week.

Yikes!

"One of the saddest lessons of history is this:
If we've been bamboozled (lied to) long enough,
we tend to reject any evidence of the bamboozle
We're no longer interested in finding out the truth.
The bamboozle has captured us.
It's simply too painful to acknowledge,
even to ourselves, that we've been taken.
Once you give a charlatan power over you,
you almost never get it back."

– *Carl Sagan*

Chapter Four

A Funny Thing Happened
on the Way to CNN

It is important to mention that in 1965, just four years before the first alleged Moon mission, political activist Ralph Nader wrote the book *Unsafe at Any Speed*, in which he detailed concise criticism of the automobile manufacturer General Motors, pointing out their numerous fatal safety shortcomings. The criticisms in Nader's book were so truthful and alarming, that congressional hearings would be conducted resulting from the revelations in his book. It was admitted at these hearings by the CEO of General Motors, James Roche himself, that Roche had hired multiple former FBI agents to follow Ralph Nader wherever he went, in order to "harass and discredit him", in an attempt to avoid the additional expense that these safety improvements would require. This extensive whistleblower tracking and harassment was done merely to save money on automobile safety upgrades. I mention this so that you realize, as the Moon landings were indeed a horrendous government and worldwide deception, and because I am a leading activist bringing the truth to the public's attention which could lead to the demise of NASA with other related agencies as well as a complete overhaul of the United States federal government, then undoubtedly at least that much spying and harassment, if not more, would be targeted by the same government at me.

It was in the late afternoon on that fateful June 30th in 1999, a Wednesday, when I found the reel of unedited material from the alleged first Moon mission, revealing that the Apollo crews never left low-Earth orbit. After having my telephone conversation about this urgent matter with whistleblower Bill Kaysing mysteriously interrupted with intrusive tones and repeated connection failures, I began to panic. I felt that Bill's life might be in danger and that I had been the cause of it.

As it was Wednesday afternoon, and I regularly attended church that evening which would be in just a couple of hours, I prepared for it and left early. At the church, I met with the elders, who already knew of this ongoing Apollo fraud film project of mine and its potential for being absolutely true. When I told them of my discovery of the astronauts faking their mission's photography, along with the audible CIA voice instructing them how to fake it, the elders told me that I had "bitten off more than I could chew" and recommended that I pass on the discovery to a more qualified institution such as CNN as soon as possible, which happened to be about a four-hour drive away.

I really did not want to give the news scoop of the century to someone else for free after all of my years of hard work and personal sacrifice in obtaining it, yet seeing how Bill's and my life might be in danger if I did not, I conceded that their advice was wise. The church meeting that evening was in a high school auditorium and it normally concluded at about nine o'clock. With three hundred or so members in attendance that evening, the parking lot was completely full at the beginning of our meeting, yet as it took extra time to wrap up the urgent discussion concerning the unique quandary that I had gotten myself into and what to safely do about it, it was about ten o'clock before one elder and I finally departed, who were the last two people and the last two cars to leave.

As I pulled out of the parking lot onto the street and ventured just a few yards past a nearby public swimming pool, which had closed when it was dark some two hours earlier, I noticed one lone car backed into the pool's driveway (as though waiting for someone and prepared for a hasty exit). This mysterious car promptly pulled out behind me as I passed by. It was obvious that whoever was in this car had been waiting for me in particular, as I was the last car of the many hundreds that had passed them by earlier, yet the only one of which received such a reaction. When I noticed the peculiar behavior of this driver, I quickly pulled my car over onto the shoulder of the road and came to a stop. I said to myself, "I'm not going anywhere until they get in front of me."

The car following me suddenly stopped right in the middle of the road behind me. The driver apparently realized that they had pulled out too quickly and had given away their covert intentions. "I've got all night. I'm not going anywhere," I said to myself. After nearly a full minute of idling in the middle of the road several yards behind me, the mysterious driver abandoned their mission and drove past me in defeat. I then remembered the words of an ancient sage about the "Art of War" who said, "Know your enemy," so I decided to turn the tables on them and followed them instead!

This mysterious driver pulled onto the highway going back towards town, so I did the same, right behind him. As it was a four-lane highway, two lanes going each direction with a median between them, I decided to pull right up along side of this vehicle to get a good look at the occupant. The first thing that I noticed was that they looked so innocuous, so normal, so un-CIA-looking. The driver was a man, about forty, wearing a sports team tank top, driving an old minivan with fuzzy dice hanging from the rearview mirror, and truly looked like the average American. Yet, when I looked into his eyes, I saw something truly frightening.

If you have ever seen a documentary about great white sharks and looked into their eyes, it is quite scary. They look soulless. They look like they don't care if your mother, wife, or child falls overboard, that they are glad to eat them all the same. This is how this man looked when I stared into his eyes. It was as if he had no soul. It was as if he would gladly kill me on command, go home, enjoy a nice dinner, and forget about me before the night's end. I had never seen anything like this before in my entire life. The scary thing is, I was about to come face-to-face with more of them.

At the very moment that we locked eyes and he gave me an unspoken threat of death, my car engine suddenly switched off. I had never experienced anything like this before either. The engine stopped running and all the lights went off, as if someone, somewhere, had pushed a button to make it all happen. I may not own any fancy cars, yet I maintain my cars meticulously, and I had never experienced anything like this in my entire life. A high-ranking ex-military intelligence officer, who was one of my top sources for my film, told me afterwards that an electromagnetic pulse must have been transmitted to my car to disable it, either from the car beside me, or perhaps even from a military satellite in Earth orbit.

All that I could do was coast to the side of the road and call the police. Unfortunately, this didn't work, as I discovered that my telephone had been simultaneously disabled. I saw that just a few yards ahead was an off ramp and I watched my adversary exit there and get back on the road onto the other side, so as to head back in my direction. Immediately thereafter, this man met up with another car on the other side of the highway, talked with them briefly through mutually rolled-down windows, and then got off at the next exit, just behind me, to loop around again and come back to where I was.

My only defense was to cross over the median on foot to the opposite side of the highway in order to best get away from them. The driver, in an attempt to follow me, then went down to the ramp he had just gotten off earlier and looped around again to the side of the road that I was now on. I then walked back to the opposite side of the highway from where I had begun, so as to get as much space between the two of us as possible. I finally started flagging down cars in a desperate attempt for aid. Sadly, despite it being obvious to passersby that I was in jeopardy, no one had the courage or compassion to help. Fortunately, a passenger-less taxi came by, and hoping for a fare, offered me a ride.

I used the taxi driver's telephone to call the police. I explained to them that I was being stalked by at least two cars and asked them to meet me in a well-known, well-lit, public area near the center of the city about ten miles away, which I only specifically identified to them when I was a minute away from it, so that any potential eavesdroppers would not have advance warning. The po-

lice stayed with me on the telephone for the entire ten-minute ride
until I arrived at the safe destination that I had picked out. As we
neared the location, my pursuers abandoned the chase. When I
met up with the police at the specified place, I notified them of
the threatening events that had just occurred and how they were
related to a revelatory journalistic matter on which I was working.
They suggested that I hire private security. The first security-mind-
ed thing which I had done between finding the revealing NASA
footage and going to church that evening, was to make several
copies of it and place them, and the original, at a few different
locations around town for safe keeping.

At this point in the evening, at about eleven o'clock, I hired
a different taxi driver (as the first was at his limit for such adventures) to take me to one of these pre-designated safe houses
for a copy of the footage, as I was a bit apprehensive to return
to the place where I had hidden the original. After I had picked
up a duplicate of the reel from there, I asked the taxi driver if he
would immediately drive me to CNN, some two hundred fifty
miles away. This driver declined the fare, yet he did take me to an
all-night restaurant where fellow taxi drivers congregated, for me
to inquire if one of them was game for such a midnight adventure.

One brave soul was willing to participate. I told him precisely
what was going on, so that he could decline the bizarre and possibly dangerous fare if he felt he needed to. I informed him that I
was a journalist making a documentary about the Moon landing
fraud and that I had just discovered previously unknown footage
of the first Apollo crew faking part of their mission. I showed him
my media credentials and the rather large professionally formatted reel as proof.

Serendipitously, this taxi driver was already of the opinion
that the Moon landings were falsified. I guess I was a little slow
to come to that realization myself. It was about two o'clock in the
morning by the time we left. As we had about a four-hour drive
ahead of us, along the way, I relayed to him the bizarre account
of what had just happened to me. I told him of finding the highly
significant reel of videotape, of the telephone conversations being

interrupted, of being followed and chased from church, and of my car being mysteriously disabled on cue.

We tried to find humor in the situation. While we kept a watchful eye to see if we were being followed, we also made jokes about it, such as when a senior citizen's bus went by, suggesting that one old lady looking out of the window at us was really wearing a mask. By the time we arrived in Atlanta Georgia, it was a little after six o'clock in the morning, Thursday, July 1, 1999. I had a colleague who worked at CNN, but they would not be in until after ten o'clock that morning, so I got the taxi driver and myself a hotel room in which to take a nap, as we both had been awake for about twenty four hours.

We woke up a little after ten o'clock that morning. I went to a pay telephone in the hotel lobby where I used my memorized AT&T access numbers to make local and long distance calls without having to insert coins that would be billed to me later. (Memorizing these emergency access numbers was the second belated security measure that I had taken.) While I was on the telephone informing the executive producer of my film (the NASA rocketry board member millionaire) of my location and precarious situation, the cab driver noticed a man repeatedly peeking his head around a nearby corner, looking at me and then concealing himself. I then telephoned CNN to get directions, as this was before GPS was widely available. The angelic taxi driver suggested that we move on as quickly as possible because of this interested third party spying on us. I took his advice and we promptly went to the parking lot and got into his taxi to depart.

As we pulled up to the edge of the hotel's parking lot where we were about to enter the street, two police cars, with lights on yet sirens off, flew past us in the parking lot and surrounded a different taxi in the circular pickup driveway in front of the hotel. As I witnessed this through the back window of our car as we drove away, I realized that they were actually after us and had mistakenly stopped the wrong taxi! I yelled, "Go! Go! Go!" and we hastily left the parking lot and drove as fast as we could to CNN.

It was disclosed about ten years ago that the United States

federal government has about as many domestic spy offices in America as there are Starbucks, or some five thousand! All you have to do is count the number of Starbucks in your town and that is how many domestic spy offices that are there as well. Scary. I have concluded that the best way to figure out what any of the Intel agencies are up to is to ask myself, "What would I do if I worked for one of these Agencies?" I was pretty sure that I was dealing with the CIA, and if I were the CIA, I would have on the secret payroll, in every town of a hundred thousand or more, several police officers, on call, to do my covert bidding. You might also call them Masons, Illuminati, or whatever. The fact is, they already have carte blanche, that is the ability as uniformed police in patrol cars, to go anywhere they want, at any time they want, under the pretense of investigating a crime.

Apparently that is precisely what happened. The CIA tracked down my whereabouts, knew that I was in a taxi leaving that particular hotel, on my way to CNN to deliver evidence that would greatly embarrass them, and they sent two of their on duty club-member cops to intercept me, who just happened to have stopped the wrong taxi in front of our hotel instead of us. Keep in mind too that none of the CIA agents had yet seen the reel of footage for themselves. They had only heard me talk about it excitedly over the telephone as "concrete proof of the Moon landing fraud", knew that I had rushed to make multiple copies of it, and had just spent four hundred dollars to urgently drive the footage in a taxi to give it to my contact at CNN, some two hundred and fifty miles away from where I lived. If I were them, I would find this alarming and do whatever I could to stop me, in order to see the condemning evidence before the CNN reporter did.

It is important to note at this point in the story, that G. Gordon Liddy, a former federal government agent (FBI) who served during the Nixon administration, once he had entered the private sector and written about his previous experiences, admitted that he once met with the CIA to discuss a plan to put liquid LSD onto the steering wheel of investigative journalist Jack Anderson, in order to either kill or discredit him. (Jack Anderson was the leading investigator at the time into the notorious Iran-Contra Presidential Scandal, wherein the CIA was caught secretly selling weapons to engage in foreign wars that were specifically prohibited by congressional legislation.) In other words, the CIA proved, long ago, that it was an organization prepared to collude with individuals within official administrations, in order to achieve mutual aims that were hidden both from the public and from the knowledge or approval of the United States Congress and Senate. After all, the Congress and Senate certainly did not *vote* to fake the Moon landings, yet NASA and the other government agencies went ahead and did it anyway. Still, no one does anything about any of this, including the recently acknowledged telephone spying on Presidents, Supreme Court Justices, and members of Congress and the Senate, done so in order to blackmail them! Amazing!

President Truman (1945-53) formed the CIA in 1947, after World War Two. He later said that establishing the CIA was the single biggest mistake of his entire presidency. Talking to Merle Miller in 1962, Truman thought that the agency had got out of hand due to a lack of oversight during the Eisenhower Presidency of 1953-1961. These are some of the comments former United States President Truman made about the CIA, when he founded:

> [It is] an organization ... that is practically equal to the Pentagon in many ways ... one Pentagon is one too many... They don't just report on wars and the like, they go out and make their own [wars] and there's nobody to keep track of what they're up to. They spend billions of dollars... It's become a government all of its own and all secret. They don't have to account to anybody. That's a very dangerous thing in a democratic society and it's got to be put a stop to. The people have a right to know what those birds are up to... The way a free government works, there's got to be a housecleaning every now and again... And when you can't do a house cleaning because everything that goes on is a damn secret, why, then we're on our way to something the Founding Fathers didn't have in mind. Secrecy and a free, democratic government don't mix...[5]

Only fifteen years after its creation (now it is more than seventy years strong) with the CIA's continual un-democratic actions, including its Moon landing fakery and other despotic criminal acts of secrecy, effectively mean that America no longer has a government of the people, by the people, for the people, as was the Founding Father's intention. A current United States senator who is a good friend of the CIA and serves on the Select Committee on Intelligence, if not secretly on the CIA's payroll as well, was even so bold as to confidently and publicly warn a United States President that he had better be careful with his criticism of the CIA, as the agency had numerous ways to retaliate against him with intensity, as President John Kennedy learned the hard way, shortly after he fired the CIA director and readied to dismantle it. When a CIA director becomes President of the United States as George Bush Senior did, and that same president reputedly "can't recall" whether or not he was in Dallas when President Kennedy was assassinated, (when every adult alive at that time in America knows exactly where they were that particular day) our country has already crossed a dangerous "Point of No Return", which in my opinion has caused our existing overwhelming tyranny.

Unfortunately at this point in my story, the CIA knew what I looked like, that I was in a taxi on my way to CNN, and that I would soon be walking through their front door with a rather large professional reel of videotape. When I arrived there, it was a little after eleven o'clock in the morning. As soon as I stepped out of the taxi and my foot hit the sidewalk in front of CNN, I was surrounded by three police officers, one of whom was a Captain. They immediately asked me (referring to the condemning videotape), "What have you got there?"

I am sure these three men had no idea what was really on this reel of videotape. They were just told to stop me from bringing it into CNN. Maybe they were told it was footage of the current president with a prostitute that would embarrass him if broadcast. I doubt if they were told the truth, so I told them the truth. I told them exactly why they were told to stop me. I told them that I was an investigate journalist who was in the possession of a reel of footage which contained the crew of Apollo 11 faking being halfway to the Moon, proving that they never left Earth orbit and consequently could not have ever walked to the Moon. I told them that this was why they were sent to intercept me, to prevent me from embarrassing NASA, the CIA and the federal Government. I showed them my driver's license as identification and my media credentials, as well as the sizable professionally formatted reel itself. "Now do you understand what you are doing here?" I asked them.

I could see that the youngest of the three policemen was horribly shocked at my disclosure and that the captain became very nervous. The third cop looked like he would kill me if given the order to do so. (He had that soulless look, just like the person who'd followed me from church the previous evening.) There were dozens of bystanders all around us, employees of CNN sitting outside on the entrance steps to eat their lunches in the nice warm weather, some of whom were curiously eying my situation. The captain was eyeing them back, doubtless contemplating what he might be able to get away with in front of so many witnesses. My taxi driver new friend got out of the car and stood beside me, in an attempt to give me back up. I asked the captain, "Am I free to go?" He would not answer the question. I asked again, "Am I free to go?" He again would not answer the question. When I took a few steps toward the front door with the condemning footage, all of the policemen simultaneously blocked my path preventing me from doing so. I asked a third time, "Am I free to go?" Again the question went deliberately unanswered.

The taxi driver, my protector, gave me a nod and a tilt of his head suggesting that we go a different direction, perhaps noticing an alternative entrance. As his advice had been right on every occasion thus far, I told the police, "Don't worry about it. We'll come back at another time that's more convenient for you. Have a nice day." I then turned away from them and followed the taxi driver, who led me down the sidewalk to the corner of the building. We looked over our shoulders and smiled at the corrupt cops as we went around the corner out of their sight. As soon as they could no longer see us, we sprinted madly down the sidewalk to get away from them. I had no idea where to go. I don't think the cab driver knew either. As I had already paid him, I quickly said goodbye with great thanks and told him to save himself and to go home, which he reluctantly did at my insistence, as he was sincerely rooting for me.

There I was, running frantically down the street in search of a backdoor to CNN. I turned another corner toward the back of the building and ran down the alley behind CNN, yet did not find an alternate entrance. As I contemplated whether or not to enter through the back door of the business on the other side of the alley, and exit through their front door in order to evade my pursuers, I apparently spent a bit too much time deciding this. In a matter of seconds, I was surrounded by what appeared to be two unmarked police cars, an unmarked van with no windows, and one motorcycle cop.

Without a word, they immediately took the videotape reel from me (a copy that I had made the previous day), handcuffed me, and opened the doors to the back of the unmarked van. Before they put me in, I heard them talking amongst themselves behind me, "Do you have *the thing?*"

"I thought you had *the thing.*"

"I don't have *the thing.* I think he's got *the thing.*"

"Oh, yeah. Here's *the thing.*"

"What *thing?*" I wondered to myself. The *thing* was a small wristband, like the kind you might receive at a concert for re-admittance. The person who handled "*the thing*" put on a pair of rubber gloves to do so, as if to not touch *the thing* directly themself. The gloved person was the one who put the mysterious plastic bracelet around one of my wrists.

At that very moment, providence arrived, in the form of a young attorney who had his tiny office entrance on the alleyway directly behind CNN, presumably to as inexpensively as possible have a "CNN Center" address. He stepped out his front door onto the alley right in front of my illegal arrest, from which he was then only a few feet away. I saw his law office sign above the door and asked him, "Are you an attorney?" He said, "Yes. I am." I said, "I would like to hire you." "What's going on?" he asked.

I promptly explained to him that I was an investigative journalist who was being illegally arrested for trying to get a reel of fake footage from the Apollo 11 mission to a personal contact at CNN. The lawyer immediately took out a notepad and started to write down my information. The cops looked at each other befuddled by his presence. I told the lawyer my name, address, the name of my film production company, the contact information of my prestigious executive producer, and the name of the NBC affiliate that I had previously worked at for two years, whose newly-appointed news director was a good friend of mine (instead of the one who had fired me for working on this news story), and whose name and contact information I also gave. The lawyer asked the police where they were taking me. The cops looked at each other confused, as if they didn't know, would not say, or now had to suddenly change their plans.

It was at this point that I suddenly became exceedingly nauseous and dizzy. Apparently *the thing* contained a skin-absorbed drug of some kind, just like G. Gordon Liddy had been on standby to use on investigative journalist Jack Anderson's steering wheel, and this is why the wristband was handled with rubber gloves and why it was placed over my wrist, where many veins were located, so as to be absorbed into my bloodstream as quickly and as strongly as possible. I had done LSD recreationally once before, about ten years earlier, and it initially felt like a heavy dose of that. So strong was the drug that I started seeing spots before my eyes and began to violently throw up. I am not sure how the conversation between the lawyer and the cops finally concluded because of the intensity of the drug, other than knowing that this sharp attorney insisted being told where I was going to be taken, as the next thing I remember, I was being put inside of the van, on my stomach, vomiting profusely.

The inside of the van was pitch black. This would have taken quite a bit of deliberate effort to have the light in the back of a van be so thoroughly blocked out that not even a sliver of light could enter. I suppose this was done for some psychological effect. Also, for such similar effect, the sound of a voice was heard in the darkness babbling in gibberish. It was a pretty comical and juvenile tactic when you think about it. I joked back at the voice and said, "If you're going to speak in tongues, then at least say some prayers on my behalf." At this remark of mine, the voice stopped and remained silent, as if they were ashamed of themselves, as I called them out on their obvious chicanery.

I'm not sure where I would have ended up, had not the assertive lawyer come to my rescue and documented what was going on, perhaps dead and mangled on a railroad track, as had happened before to a NAA employee Thomas Baron who would not cooperate with the Apollo cover up. Another attorney later informed me of a great and dangerous loophole that the Nazis used to employ in the legal system of habeas corpus, which is the law that an arrestee must be brought before a judge within forty-eight hours of their arrest, in order to determine whether or not such a detention is legal, and if this is not done, the person arrested can never be charged for the alleged offence again. However, if a person is instead declared "*potentially* insane", by anyone, they are thereby *technically* not under arrest, rather under "*observation*" (though equally have their freedom taken away) and can then be locked up for *five times longer*, or ten days instead of two, *without* having an arrestee's rights to a telephone call or legal counsel, as they are, *technically*, not under "arrest". Clever!

Even though the United States federal government would collect about twenty percent more money from a federal sales tax of ten percent than that of their citizen's income tax, and in the process, the elimination of the costly Internal Revenue Service would save the country over one hundred billion dollars every ten years, corrupt leaders of this country keep the IRS in place anyway, as a "legal" Nazi loophole attack dog, to go after the government's political dissenters. In the same way, even though freedom of the press and freedom of speech are supposed to be the law of the land, I discovered the hard way that designating whistleblowers as *crazy and locking them up* to prevent them from sounding the alarm, is another one of the government's sly tactics to go after those who are bringing their crimes into the light. We have to remember that Nazi Germany was called democratic too, with their citizens "voting" all of the time.

Had it not been for the lawyer's timely intervention these unknown government agents who illegally arrested me and might have otherwise just disposed of me, were now instead forced to adopt the best legal option available to them. This option was not detaining me in custody, as they had no legal cause to do so, rather to throw me into a psychiatric hospital for ten days as a "crazy" person. Not only would this stop me from giving my reel of fake Apollo footage to my journalistic contact at CNN, it would give them enough time to analyze the reel for themselves and calculate a response.

My kidnappers then drove me to the psychiatric ward at the Atlanta General Hospital, which was likely not where they had first intended, yet it was where they informed the lawyer I would now be taken. Rather than driving the van to the front entrance where patients were normally dropped off, they deliberately parked some considerable distance away. I was about to discover that this was so that they could have time to interrogate me first. They pulled me out of the van, strapped me into a wheelchair, and very slowly wheeled me to the hospital, clearly done so as to increase the time with which they could ask me a prepared set of questions, specifically intended for someone under the influence of whatever drug they had illegally given me. Even in my drugged state I could see that they were reading off a printed list pinned to a clipboard. It was beginning to look as if this whole operation had been prearranged well in advance.

The very first question they asked me was, "Where is your son." I had at the time a two and a half year old son. I was divorced and had custody of him on weekends. When I found the alarming footage and was subsequently chased on the highway in the middle of the night, I had immediately telephoned my ex-wife (who supported the argument that my film makes at the time we were married) and told her what was going on. Working on my

"What would I do if I were the CIA?" premise, I had concluded that they might kidnap my son for the ransom of the videotape, so after my discovery of the condemning Apollo footage and my subsequent telephone call about it with Bill Kaysing was mysteriously interrupted, I had urgently asked my ex-wife to take our son, leave her home at once, and go to an unpredictable location. She had immediately done so.

I am not sure what drug these government agents had illegally given me, yet it had the effect of "truth serum". Under its influence I thought that these men were the "good guys" trying to help me, so I told them absolutely everything they wanted to know. (Consequently, government torture is never necessary and is only used as unethical retaliation.) The next thing my interrogators asked me was, "Where did you get the footage?" I told them that too. I was drugged up so much that I do not remember the rest of the questions or the answers I gave them. I did recall later that it was Thursday morning, July 1, 1999, when they checked me into that locked wing of the hospital, where they then placed me in a large comfortable chair, wherein I immediately fell fast asleep.

The drugs that they had administered to me in the alley were so severe that I slept for more than twenty four hours. When I finally woke up at about four o'clock in the afternoon it was Friday, July 2nd. I found myself still sitting in the same chair. The facility was quite modern. They served quality orange juice and peanut butter crackers as snacks and had a courtesy telephone for detainees. I first got to know one of the nurses as politely and promptly as I could, got to the point to where I felt that I could trust her, and then asked her kindly if she could please tell me how long my stay was expected to be. She informed me that I would be in their facility for a *minimum* of ten days. I thanked her and headed over to the telephone. Armed with my emergency AT&T long distance access codes which I had memorized for just such an occasion as this, I proceeded to telephone the executive producer of the film, as well as the new trustworthy news director at the television station where I used to work, to inform them both of my unusual situation.

The executive producer of the film found the predicament both alarming and amusing. I guess he was just as dumbfounded by it as I was and he cleverly used humor to relieve the tension. After about twenty minutes or so on the phone, accomplishing several important calls and making real progress in the matter, I suddenly heard drilling coming from the exact opposite side of the wall that the telephone was on. Really! Some spook (spy) had been sent, likely dressed up as a telephone repairman, to literally yank the telephone line I was using out of the wall!

A moment later the phone call I was on got disconnected and then I received a tap on the shoulder from a nurse, whom I had not seen before, who said that I was immediately being transferred to another facility, right after I had just been told that I would be there for ten days and had just informed all of my telephone contacts the very same thing. I asked this nurse, "When is this going to occur?" She replied, "Right away." I told her that the other nurse had just informed me that I was going to remain there for ten days. This new nurse said that all of that had been suddenly changed. When I asked "Why?" She replied, "None of your business." Learning to take all of this in my stride, I calmly put the disconnected telephone back on the receiver and walked over to the window of the nurse's station, where the nurse I trusted was sitting, and asked her, "Who was it that made the decision to suddenly transfer me to another facility?" She responded, "Some new doctor I have never seen before. Today is his first day." Yikes!

They then handcuffed me and loaded me into the back of another van, this one was not so dark, and I sat in it for nearly an hour and a half, while it was driverless with the engine running. The long delay made me think that higher ups were carefully deciding my fate. When the driver finally got in, I saw that with his quarter inch haircut he looked more like an old drill sergeant than a low-level hospital employee. I asked him where he was taking me. The driver did not reply, as if hadn't heard me. I asked him a few other questions for the first thirty minutes of the ride, to which he also never replied, as if I was not there.

I was not sure where I was being taken, yet it was obviously well outside of the city, as it took over an hour to arrive there. By the time I ended up at the new destination, it was dark. The place where they had taken me looked like a prison for the criminally insane, with intense barbed wire fencing all around it. I could tell that it was a very secure facility and that once I entered the interior locked-down section, that there was no hope of escape. Fortunately for me, the place was arranged in multiple pods, with exterior covered walkways between them. The first place they took me to was the reception building. There I was registered and de-handcuffed. The driver then left and an orderly proceeded to escort me out of that building down a covered walkway outside to an adjacent pod.

I quickly estimated that the walk between the two buildings would only last about twenty seconds. I took advantage of the short time by promptly asking my escort about the laws and rules governing my detainment. "Can I use the telephone?" "Can I speak with a lawyer?" "How long will I be here?" He seemed a bit annoyed with the questions and finally replied in exasperation, "I don't know. I'm just doing my job." My last words to him were, "And so am I." I then ran off the walkway and into the thick night fog of the prison yard to begin my escape.

I could tell that the building that I was about to enter was very secure and that this brief interlude in the open air would be my only opportunity for liberation. I figured quite rightly that the hourly employee who was escorting me had no desire to chase after me into the night and the thick fog. I quickly found my way to the fence and climbed over it and all the barbed wire, as if my son's life depended on it. I figured the CIA's goal was to get me and my two-year old son simultaneously, so as to force a trade with the original footage. Subsequently, I believed that my escape would thwart that scenario and protect my son. Once over the barbed wire at the top of the tall fence, and on the ground, I made my way down a remote country road. When I saw a patrolling po-lice car a short time later, I made my way down a steep ravine into a creek and from then on used it as my pathway, rightly figuring that a policeman, Illuminati member or not, was not about to leave his comfortable car and ford a deep creek in the middle of the night to search for a "missing psychiatric patient".

I had no idea where I was or which direction to go, so I humorously decided to follow the Moon. Fortunately, I was a healthy thirty-four year-old at the time and had a lot of extra adrenaline, plus the undying drive to protect the life of my toddler son. When the creek water smelled fine, I drank it. When it smelled funky, I did not. Sometimes the creek was so deep that I had to swim through it. At other times wading in it up to my knees.

At sunrise I came to an old gas station with the Christian "fish" symbol on it. I can tell you now, that during that entire strange experience, I had never been closer to God in my entire life, not in an apocalyptic way, rather in a full of joy and purposeful way. I was living with a clear conscience. How fitting that true Christians and their "fish" symbol would be my salvation that day. The kind people who owned the gas station let me use their telephone as much as I wanted and offered me much needed food and water. I then telephoned a good friend, who knew that my film was truthful and also happened to live Atlanta. This person very kindly came and collected me, and then drove for six hours to get me back home.

I didn't realize it at the time, until someone pointed it out to me, that I looked like I had been flogged by ancient Romans. I had cuts, bruises, and abrasions all over my face and up and down both sides of my arms, from the barbed wire and the countless thorn bushes that I had forged through, although I was completely oblivious to the pain at the time. I bore the scars from this ordeal for about six months afterwards. From this experience I quickly realized that fighting the CIA was futile and that if my movements were going to be monitored, they might as well be monitored from the comfort of my home.

Upon later investigation, there was no record of my arrest in Atlanta, no record of my stay at any hospital there, and no APB (all-points-bulletin) for an escaped "psychiatric patient". I did have the remnants of some exotic government drug in my system though, so I urinated in a cup and had a friend take it to a reputable laboratory for examination, to prove that the CIA had illegally drugged me with some mysterious truth serum agent. When I contacted the lab to hear the results of the test, they informed me that an overnight break in had occurred and that the only thing the thieves had taken was my urine specimen. So many coincidences.

This account is my first public testimony that I have ever given about these strange espionage adventures of mine, which must read like scenes from a movie, yet they indeed did happen. I had refrained from talking about them publicly earlier, because I reasoned that saying the United States government and its agencies really did stage the greatest event in the history was peculiar sounding enough. However, as this book will likely be my only biography, I figured that for posterity's sake I had better tell the world exactly what happened.

A funny thing *really did* happen on the way to CNN.

**"It is easier to fool people
than to convince them that they have been fooled."**

– *Mark Twain*

Chapter Five

A Funny Thing Happened
on the Way to Church

I arrived home from my adventures in Atlanta in the early afternoon on Saturday, July 3, 1999. I was exhausted. I slept for about twenty hours, waking on Sunday morning, July 4th, at about ten o'clock. Seeing how it was Independence Day (my favorite holiday as a true American patriot) and a Sunday as well, the church that I was attending at that time was holding a special outdoor afternoon service at two o'clock in a local park. As I was still a little uneasy staying at home all by myself, considering what had just occurred, I decided to go for a drive in a car I had borrowed from a friend until the service commenced. (My own car was still abandoned on the side of the road after it had been disabled by that malfunction which occurred the preceding Wednesday night, when I had driven up alongside my mysterious stalker so as to get a good look at him).

At this point, after such unusual happenings, I was just a little paranoid. When I pulled out of my driveway and made it to the first major street that Sunday morning, I wondered if there really were more white government-looking cars with their lights turned on around me than usual, or was this just a coincidence? I decided that the safest thing for me to do was to keep moving and to stay in populated public places. The city that I lived in had an interstate loop around it, so I just kept driving in circles around downtown, figuring that there would always be a lot of people around me and that there were continual exits with populated gas stations and restaurants.

Were there two white cars with their lights on that kept making the repeated loops with me? It seemed like it, or were my senses overly heightened because of my recent bizarre experiences, or possibly both? When I began to think that I was not imagining it and slowed down to get a closer look at one of the two cars that seemed to be following me, at that very moment, my borrowed car's engine mysteriously switched off, just like my own had done a few days earlier! This time however, I was right at the busiest off-ramp in the city and I managed to coast to a stop at a popular gas station where there were a number of people.

Fortunately this time, the car started back up after it had rested awhile. I did notice however, when I looked at the car's engine, that all of the brake fluid was drained out and that the dashboard brake fluid warning light indicator had been intentionally disconnected. After buying some brake fluid from the gas station and filling it up, I decided to head over to the church's outdoor service early, figuring that someone would be there beforehand to help set up for it. As I suspected, a few people who I knew were already there helping to organize the event, yet I did not bother them with the details of my recent adventures. For the moment, I kept this to myself and just helped them prepare for the coming service.

When my closest friend in the church arrived, he helped me calm down and logically assess the situation. He was aware of my current film production and knew that it was absolutely true even before I did, as one of his relatives had been a top White House advisor to a two-term President who had privately acknowledged the Moon landing deception. At this point, I stopped caring that my actions were being monitored by the CIA, after all, what could I do about it but nothing? At the same time I couldn't help but notice all of the curious things happening to me and marvel at them with an increasing sense of humor.

My good friend kept a watchful eye on our surroundings, all the while trying to help me relax. Although it was a better option than staying home alone, I was still a little concerned that with an outdoor church service in a public park, which had so many unknown visitors, the location could easily be infiltrated by my adversaries. As I had already been illegally drugged by skin contact, I was reluctant to shake hands with any people that I did not know. My astute friend noticed one unknown woman in particular who made a beeline straight toward me from quite a distance away. Coincidentally, she immediately wanted to shake my hand. I played it safe and politely ignored her gesture to do so. She was determined and tried to get me to shake hands several times thereafter, attempts which I also politely ignored.

This woman was petite and spoke to me with a slight, yet noticeable, eastern European accent. Having had a little prior experience from similar adventures in East Berlin, back when the Wall was still in place, her accent was discernable to my ear. (The recounting of those adventures will have to wait for another occasion). So, with this knowledge in mind, I asked her where she was from. She said Ohio, which was coincidentally where I was from. I asked her if she was born there, and she said "yes", though her accent made that seriously doubtful. I asked her if she had any relatives from Eastern Europe or anywhere near there from whom she might have learned to speak. She replied "no". To this my friend and I just looked at each other in cautious and curious bewilderment and then we made an excuse to move away from her company. This was not turning into a normal Sunday or July 4th celebration day that's for sure.

Unfortunately for me, the pastor of the church I was attending at that time, was new and I believe this might have even been his first service. He certainly had no previous relationship with me nor with any of the elders in the church, who already knew that my predicament was genuine and serious. When the new pastor heard through the grapevine that it was alleged that the CIA was following one of his members because he was investigating the authenticity of the Moon landings, he immediately rolled his eyes in disbelief. He said that I should be swiftly checked into a mental hospital, all the while arrogantly rebuking the elders, whom he didn't even know, for taking me seriously. (I laugh now as I write this.) This minister would later be fired by the very same elders for being so arrogant, nevertheless at that time, he led my church congregation.

I had asked the advice of my best friend in the church as to his opinion on this matter. He figured, as I appeared to be hopelessly surrounded by superior adversaries who knew well where I lived and moved, that I actually might be safer under the constant observation of the staff of a psychiatric hospital, because it would at least have good security and contain numerous objective third-party eyewitnesses.

I was rather disheartened that as soon as I told the new pastor that I would submit to his leadership out respect for my understanding of the Scriptures at that time, which seemed to suggest this, that without hesitation he immediately notified the park police to come and take me away to the local General Hospital's psychiatric ward... yet again. Once I arrived there, I was handcuffed to a hospital bed – after all, you can't have people who question their government's integrity running freely about! Shortly after I was handcuffed, once again I began to feel under the influence of another strong drug, even though I thought I had been very careful about who and what I touched. How I got drugged this second time was a total mystery to me. I suppose that as I was again wrongfully admitted into such a place, that the purpose of the drug was to make me "loopy", so that I would better fit the characteristics of a mentally ill person.

At the hospital I noticed a seemingly elderly woman sitting in a wheelchair positioned near the entrance to my room, who seemed to take an undue interest in my situation. When I was later transferred to another facility, there she was again, hovering by the entrance to my room a second time, right as the nurse assigned to me took my preliminary information. I told him precisely what was going on in exacting detail. I also showed him my identification and media credentials. As I did so, you could see the expression on his face was one of sobering realization that what I was saying was true. I not only told him about the two recent occasions in which I had been drugged against my will, I also told him how this same woman in the wheelchair promptly followed me from one institution to the other, and how in both cases, she was giving me undue attention, as if trying to eavesdrop on the conversations that I was having with the medical staff.

All that this nurse had to do was look over his shoulder to discover that this woman, who had followed me from the first hospital to the second one, and who was constantly hanging out at the entrance to my room at both locations, was indeed right there at the doorway, attempting to listen in on our private conversation. When the nurse agreed that this was quite suspicious, he went over to her and insisted that she vacate the location. The woman acted as if she did not understand him, replying in gibberish. The nurse then asked this woman again to leave the doorway to my room, and yet she persisted to stay there, again acting like she did not understand him. When the nurse then signaled to two bouncer-like orderlies to remove her from the entrance to my room, suddenly this mysterious woman understood him completely and immediately wheeled herself away.

As my lengthy story took sometime to communicate to the nurse, after about five more minutes into it, I noticed this strange woman was still in my line of sight, though at some distance away, she was still curiously peering into my room at the two of us. When the nurse looked to confirm this, and agreed that this was very strange and inappropriate behavior, he signaled to the two orderlies again, this time to remove her from that location as well, which they did. After another five minutes or so, I noticed that this mysterious woman had left an electronic device of some kind on the floor, in the very place she had just vacated, pointing precisely in our direction. My new nurse-friend found this equally surprising and out of the ordinary. He went over to the object and found out that it was a small tape recorder with a directional microphone!

The office of the administrator in charge of the facility happened to be nearby. After finding the tape recorder the nurse went over to him and they talked at some length about my unique situation in the entrance to the office. The man in charge listened intently, looked over at the strange woman several times, stepped into his office to get a clipboard, which apparently had this other patient's information on it, and once outside again, scratched his head in perplexity about something. The nurse showed the administrator the tape recorder belonging to the woman, as well as my media credentials, who then nodded, apparently having been aware of my work at the local NBC affiliate, as I had recently appeared on camera in news broadcasts.

At about this time, two individuals in black business suits came up to them both and interrupted their conversation. These two new men tilted their heads in my direction, as if referring to me, and then quickly dismissed the nurse and ushered the administrator back into his office for a private conversation with him. The hospital administrator cast a terrified look in my direction before all three went inside his office, shutting the door behind them. I do not know who these two men were or what they talked about for roughly fifteen minutes, yet when the door was opened and the two strange visitors exited, the administrator looked as if he had seen a ghost.

Later that evening (it was actually at about one-thirty the following morning) two different mysterious men entered my room. This time they were wearing hospital scrubs, the kind that you would *expect* employees to wear in such a facility. Unbeknownst to them, the place that I was in was so "modern" that none of their employees actually wore such formal hospital attire. They dressed in plain street clothes instead. These two strange late night visitors woke me up and said, "Mr. Sibrel. We would like to talk with you." I said, "I'm all ears." They insisted that we not talk in my room, as if they did not trust it as a secure place to have a private conversation, and took me some distance away to the deserted employee cafeteria.

Once we arrived there, these two strangers took my temperature, my blood pressure, and asked me what kind of medicine the hospital was giving me. While I told them that I wasn't receiving any medication, I thought to myself, "If they really worked here, wouldn't they already know what medication they were giving me?" During the discussion these two secretive men kept encouraging me with words like, "You're doing great Mr. Sibrel, hang in there" and "We're all rooting for you." I wondered what in the world they meant by such remarks. They seemed genuinely concerned for my well being, as if we were comrades in some battle.

I looked at them more closely and noted that one of the men was about twenty six, with a really short military-style hair cut, and the other, who seemed to be in charge, also had a military-styled haircut and was about forty. As I was looking them over, wondering who they were and what they were up to, I noticed that the older man was wearing a watch with a "United States Marines" insignia. Just as I was about to ask him about his watch, a little voice inside of me told me not to, so I followed my intuition about this, remained silent, and just listened to what they had to say.

I cannot tell you everything that they discussed with me, as I made a pledge not to, yet let me make a few things clear. I was made aware that the white cars that I had seen on the interstate driving with their lights on near me, when I was on my way to church after my harrowing escape in Atlanta, were best described as "the good guys", sent there for my protection. More importantly, I was informed that the United States has been engaged in an unpublicized civil war for a very long time, perhaps since the end of the American Civil War, or perhaps beginning at President Kennedy's assassination by the CIA. In any case, two or more factions within the federal government's many secretive agencies have been fighting each other for quite some time. I don't mean just arguing, I mean actual fighting; literally killing one another, and that there is a "gentlemen's agreement" among all parties involved not to publicize this internal civil war.

Like most universal conflicts, it boils down to good versus evil. Unfortunately in this case, the "bad guys" are masquerading on the public scene as the good guys, which is their ultimate clever disguise, like the insidiousness of pedophile priests who run orphanages, taking grotesque advantage of the innocent under their care, all the while having the undeserved reputation as society's purest saviors. Likewise, those most ridiculed by the CIA-run propaganda news media, are often the very ones who are trying the hardest to expose their corruption. In my opinion, many people who go out of their way to defend the Apollo astronauts as if they are cherished heroes, end up attacking people like myself, who only want the uncaught criminals who instigated this hidden fraud to be brought to justice. Many naïve CIA-media-deceived people do not realize what traitors to our nation so many presidents and government officials are, all the while these hardened criminals receive the adoration and financial support from the very people they are manipulating, enslaving, and eventually exterminating with their nefarious selfish schemes.

I was informed that each of these warring factions within the US government have their own secret armies, air forces, reconnaissance satellites, and spies, which are continually battling each other, under the radar and outside the reporting of the media. How it all will end I do not know. I do know that President Kennedy's assassination, the Apollo deception, as well as certain other events like 9/11, are all manifestations of this internal battle. When three thousand professional architects and engineers sign a petition, risking their lifelong careers and reputations to emphatically state that the twin towers at the World Trade Center (WTC) could in no way collapse due to aircraft or miscellaneous debris fires, and yet not a single thing is done about this in the twenty years that followed, then there is something very wrong with the United States federal government, proving that these dark evil forces are the ones running the show, and that they have been doing so for quite some time. In fact, due to the CIA's complete media control, very few people are even aware that there was a *third* skyscraper that collapsed on 9/11, that was not even hit by an airplane, which was known as WTC "Building 7". Because this third high-rise building was *not* hit by an airplane, *yet collapsed anyway*, this third lesser-known skyscraper collapse on 9/11 is not publicized by the CIA-run media, as it proves beyond a doubt that explosive demolitions were used that day, exposing the propagated lie that "foreign terrorists" were responsible, rather than *domestic* government ones.

After my hour or so discussion with my two new friends in the hospital's employee cafeteria, I was escorted back to my room, now filled with surprising new information and a profound new purpose. The next day, or rather later that morning, just as I had previously followed the person following me in my epic car chase, I was now tasked with spying on the people who were spying on me in the hospital, the ones posing as patients. I immediately noticed that the woman "patient" in the wheelchair, who had followed me from one facility to another, and who was continually trying to eavesdrop on my conversations with the staff, was regularly talking with another "patient" in particular, a woman a few years her younger. They both had that same soulless look in their eyes as the man who had chased after me from church earlier in the week, one of a cold heartless shark who would relish eating me for dinner.

I am really not confrontational by nature, as some might wrongly believe after watching *Astronauts Gone Wild*, in which I challenged eight Apollo astronauts face-to-face about their fraud. At the same time, I am not afraid to be confrontational when justice is at stake and I know for certain that I am on the right side of it. Such is the case with this particular project of mine. It does not bother me in the least that the majority of Americans think that the Moon landings were real. I am satisfied with the twenty-five percent of them who recognize the hard plain truth, as well as the half or more of the rest of the world who have already acknowledged this deception. History is replete with forward-thinking individuals who were ahead of their time, who were ridiculed by their contemporaries yet praised by future generations. In fact one might ask if, historically, when has the majority *ever* been right the first time? In the case of these two adversaries of mine disguised as fellow patients, it was the knowledge of all of the foregoing facts that emboldened me to personally confront them.

I nicknamed the older one in the wheelchair "the supervisor", as she seemed to be the leader of the two. Although this woman always talked coherently with her counterpart, whenever I, or a member of the staff would address her, she would switch to gibberish, in keeping with her cover as a psychiatric patient. Quite comical really. As such, I ended up having a lot of fun with them, something which they were not used to and it seemed to frustrate and irritate them.

The younger of the pair of suspicious "patients" who did speak to others kept asking me for the date and time of my sanity court hearing, as it was my plan to show this newly-discovered footage of Apollo 11 fake photography in court as my defense. (It was the law of my home state that within a week of incarceration a judge had to determine whether or not an incarcerated patient was "a harm to themselves or others".) As it had only been a matter of a few days since a copy of the reel was confiscated by the CIA in Atlanta, there may not yet have been time for it to have been properly reviewed and discussed by the "higher-ups" therein. The idea of premiering the footage in a public court of law before such a time might have made my opposition a little nervous. Subsequently, there followed persistent questioning from this "patient" as to the date and time of my court hearing. After several days of being repeatedly asked this question, and not really knowing what difference it would make, I finally gave in to this woman's persistent query and told her my court date and time. Well, it seemingly did make a difference. "Coincidentally", on the very day and hour of my court appearance, the courthouse caught on fire, postponing my hearing. So many coincidences, so little time.

I am not sure what protocol was broken, yet for some strange reason (I believe that it had something to do with my late night "good guy" visitors) soon after that I was released, ahead of schedule and without a court hearing. I went home, rested, and tried as best as I could to put these strange events behind me. Sometime later, my late night clandestine military visitors, or their close associates, forwarded to me a scan of an actual classified internal White House document from the 1960s, in which the faking of the Moon landing was formally discussed. There it was **in writing** and on my computer screen. As I was already exhausted from my many recent espionage adventures, I saved the document for later review.

The following day I started to have internet connection problems and had to call the service provider, who promptly sent over a "repairman". This turned out to be a person who just so happened to have moved next door to me the previous week – coincidence! He insisted, in a way that I have never seen before under any circumstance, that I needed to give him my computer's master password in order to troubleshoot the problem, which had only begun *after* I received this incriminating White House document. I told the "repairman" that I would type my computer's master password in myself in the appropriate window. As I readied my fingers over the keyboard to do so, there he was, looking over my shoulder attempting to read my password as I typed it! When I insisted that he leave the room while I entered it, he did, and I closed the door behind him. As I again prepared to enter my master password, I looked over my shoulder and found that he had opened a crack in the nearby door and had his eye peering through it, directly looking at my keyboard!

When his second attempt failed at getting my password, the "repairman" then hooked up his military grade laptop to my computer and insisted that I use it to enter my computer's master password "while he looked the other way". (Obviously my password could then be recorded on his laptop.) When I refused, he said that my internet connection would not be fixed unless I followed his privacy invading commands. I said, "That's fine. I'll just find another company that is easier to work with," and sent him on his way. When I contacted the new service provider, presuming that is whom I was *really* connected to on the telephone, they also unprecedentedly asked me for my computer's master password in order to connect internet services with them! When I pointed out to this anonymous person on the other end of the telephone that I had used their company before at a different location and was never asked for my computer's master password, plus the fact that I had even been notified in an email from this company that a *real* employee of theirs would *never* ask for such a thing, my call with them was abruptly disconnected.

While I again began to think that I needed to start scrambling all of my telephone and internet communications in order to safely investigate the Moon landing fraud any further, my late night "good guy" liaisons instructed me not to, because encryption software is frequently updated to overcome newly-advanced decoding, and this might make it more difficult for them to protect me. Apparently both the good guys and the bad guys are constantly monitoring what I am up to regarding my unfolding investigation into this monumental federal government-changing revelation, and that the best thing for me to do, for my own safety, is to conduct most of my business about this out in the open for both parties to see.

I am now free to disclose all of this information because my twenty-year confidentiality agreement with these good men has recently expired. When I was first introduced to them in July of 1999, my realization that I was continually being monitored by the bad guys went from being an alarming life-threatening predicament, to an amusing comical spy adventure worthy of a Hollywood feature film.

"Tell my people their transgression."

– *Isaiah 58:1*

Chapter Six

NBC News Agrees that the Moon Landings Were Faked

After I had rested from my "X-Files" adventures, and seeing how an old friend was just installed as the news director at the NBC station from where I had previously been fired for working on the Moon landing fraud investigation, I thought that I would give my friend and this familiar network the opportunity to be the first to broadcast my discovery of the reel of unedited outtakes from the first mission, along with its CIA prompting audio, which proves that the Apollo 11 crew never left low-Earth orbit. I had known and worked with this news director for over two years when he was the producer of the news program on which I worked. We had mutual respect for each other's work and also enjoyed each other's company.

I remember the day very well, when, together with the executive producer of my film, we met privately in the news director's office and showed him this incredibly revealing footage for the very first time. The NBC news director turned pale white, clasped his hand over his mouth in astonishment, and fell back in his chair as if he had just heard that President Kennedy had been shot. After a while he sighed and said, **"This proves we didn't go to the Moon."**

"I know," I said, "What do we do about it?"

The NBC news director thought quietly for quite a long time and then finally said, **"I cannot broadcast this. It will cause a civil war. I will not be responsible for that."** I disagreed, saying that American citizens discovering that the already well-known corrupt government agencies had added the faking of the Apollo Moon landings to their list of many recognizable frauds against the people of the United States would cause a civil war, in that Americans would not be fighting against one another as a result of such an unpalatable disclosure, rather their corrupt leadership. I suggested that instead it would instigate a rather dramatic, much-needed overhaul of all government agencies. Nevertheless, he could not be persuaded out of his decision. The news director said that he was sorry and I left feeling rather hopeless. Quite a country US citizens live in when the news media is afraid to broadcast the true account of an event because it is *too truthful.*

What would our Founding Fathers and Mothers say? What would the public say? Wouldn't they want to know the truth about the vast corruption overseen by their own government and the misappropriation of the equivalent of two hundred billion dollars? What would they say if they knew that the trusted professional news media deliberately withheld information about such a vast distortion and misrepresentation of the most significant event of the 20th Century, the continued concealment of which only emboldens the perpetrators of such an event to carry out even more horrendous crimes against the US public in the future?

This would not be the first time that NBC or the news media would deliberately neglect their duty to their own people regarding this and other monumental historic matters, which they deliberately withheld from the public for fear of a righteous rebellion of the citizenry against their corrupt government overlords, with whom the mainstream media have become directly complicit as their bedfellow agents. Just before he was assassinated – in my opinion by the CIA, and a CIA-loving replacement was put in his place – President Kennedy said that not only was government secrecy "repugnant", but that it was *specifically the news media's responsibility to question and criticize the government as a safeguard to freedom.* This is precisely why the Founding Fathers wrote *"Freedom of the Press".* Yet when proof of one of the greatest known government frauds is presented to them, and they acknowledge it as being true, it is nevertheless *deliberately* withheld from the public! How can the press be described as *free* (independent) when – demonstrably in order to protect the status quo and the criminal perpetrators – it has bowed to the extremely dangerous and biased agendas of the CIA and likeminded corrupt agencies and corporations.

The United States military, or rather the Pentagon, had to admit on September 10, 2001, that after an independent investigation, it had "misplaced" two thousand three hundred billion dollars ($2.3 trillion) over the preceding few years, slyly promising that it would look into the matter immediately. Not so coincidentally, the very next day, the same Pentagon conducted a training exercise of the World Trade Center buildings being struck by airplanes, all the while two of the World Trade Center buildings really were "coincidentally" being simultaneously struck by two aircraft. Thinking that it was part of the exercise, the nation's Air Defense Command was intentionally standing down, thus critically delaying their timely response against the real perpetrators of the attack. Thereafter the CIA's media was completely directed on the aftermath of 9/11, making any investigation of the government's missing 2.3 trillion dollars, that was only mentioned once, and just the day before, completely forgotten, simply because the public was deliberately never reminded of it by the complicit government-controlled news media.

My point is that if the military had an extra $2.3 trillion back in 2001 (and likely more now), money which they did not have to account for (and what use is money unless you spend it), then we should be asking, "What has the federal government secretly purchased with this vast sum of money in order to increase its power in the world and at home?" A single ship in the Navy, an aircraft carrier, costs thirteen billion dollars. At about half that cost, CNN was sold for only seven billion dollars. Supposing that in order to control public opinion the CIA had decided to *covertly* add CNN to its list of media assets, that would still leave twenty-two hundred and ninety-three billion dollars of spending money.

It is a little known, yet acknowledged fact, that Google was founded with financing from the CIA, obviously for the purpose of tracking the private opinions of citizens and controlling the information which they receive.[6]

What about the rest of social media? What about AT&T and the other communications companies? What about ABC, NBC, CBS, *Time* magazine, the *New York Times*, and all the others? Every single one of these could have already been purchased by the Pentagon and their intelligence (information) agencies many years ago with their admitted "misplaced" trillions of dollars, plus the continual profits from these businesses, which would add to their available funds for untold future control and potential secret telecommunication and social media purchases. As the CIA admitted more than fifty years ago that the agency regularly purchases businesses and hires token CEOs to mask their secret ownership of them, I have no doubt that some or *all* of this has already happened.[7]

This is **precisely why** *one hundred percent* of *one thousand five hundred* mainstream media outlets surveyed fully supports the CIA-initiated overthrow of the **democratically elected** government of Venezuela, *thusly* **one hundred percent of them** are under the direct ownership or control of the CIA.

This is precisely why multi-billion-dollar corporations and their government counterparts wrote the deregulation legislation which permits all of these "news" outlets to be owned by a *single* entity, and thereafter consolidated all television networks, magazines, and newspapers into *central* ownership with *identical* information which are then disseminated, from the top down, to the public. Prior to this sly, barely noticed deregulation, it was forbidden for one individual or company to own more than two media outlets at the same time, in order to insure a free (independent) press. Today, *ninety-five percent* of all news media is operated by just *six* multi-billion-dollar corporations, which are likely directly owned or controlled by the CIA and their complicit counterparts. The purpose of this is to control your *perception* of reality, *not* to offer you reality, as the Moon landing deception is the perfect example.

Simply put, news corruption means nothing but lies therefrom, or the *exact opposite of the truth*. If the corrupt CIA's mainstream media continually praises one government leader, then no doubt the *truth* is that this individual is *really* highly corrupt. If the CIA's mainstream media continually criticizes another government leader, then it must be that this one is trying to expose their corruption. It is that simple and that bad. (By the way, the mainstream media was highly critical of President Kennedy, *because he exposed corruption*, and when their lies about him could not bring him down, a bullet was used instead.) If the same CIA-run news media at one time falsely claimed that cigarettes *improved* your health, when the *exact opposite was true*, then what about the latest modern medicines they are pushing today? Could it be that, in fact, the latest medical cure that the CIA's mainstream media is daily espousing as beneficial, *actually* makes a person sicker? In a world where ticker-tape parades were held for the "heroic" astronauts whose pre-created, staged Moon walks were imaged in highly-secure and secret film studios, I am sorry to say that such modern day deceptions could very well be taking place... **now.**

As someone who worked as a senior editor in television news for two years, I can testify to this fact. We referred to our broadcast as a *show*, not news, simply because it was completely controlled from the top down like any corporation, where the anchors (readers) simply regurgitate the scripted words from unseen superiors. Don't believe me? Please watch the short, yet very revealing clip below and notice the network logos in the lower part of the screen (left and right), which reveal that *all* of the major networks (ABC, NBC, CBS, FOX) are receiving the *very same* scripts from a *central*, high level source. *Independent* news on network television? Sadly, it's not anywhere to be found, see **Sibrel.com** Moon Man link #5.

While the naïve studio audience being shown these synchronized broadcasts laughed at the reality of the outrageousness of this blatant *centralized* control of propaganda masquerading as "news", when I watched this segment myself for the very first time, my heart sank, as I was truly horrified as to the degree to which the average citizen is subjected to these *daily* deceitful and deliberate manipulations, done so to control what people *think*, and thereby, control their *actions*. In 1977 the highly respected and

Pulitzer Prize winning Watergate reporter Carl Bernstein had this to say about exactly who it is who has *central* control over the public's information:

More than four hundred American journalists have secretly carried out assignments for the Central Intelligence Agency, according to documents on file at CIA headquarters. In many instances, CIA documents show that journalists were contracted to perform covert missions for the CIA with the consent of the managers of America's leading news organizations. Among the executives who lent their cooperation to the CIA, were the heads of *Time* magazine, *Newsweek, the New York Times*, ABC, NBC, CBS, the Associate Press, United Press International, and Reuters.[8]

I think that just about covers everyone around at that time. Keep in mind that Bernstein was writing this way back in 1977, when it was illegal for anyone to own more than two news outlets at the same time. Today just six entities, allegedly independent from one another, own at least ninety-five percent of the current "news" (false propaganda) outlets. Seeing how this alarming discovery of the CIA-controlling the news media was made more than forty years ago, I suspect now that the number of journalists on the CIA's payroll might be one hundred times higher than the four hundred reported at that time. CNN, FOX, MSNBC, USA Today, and many others, were not on this secretive CIA list simply because they did not exist at the time of Carl Bernstein's discovery. I am sure by now that all of these corporations are also highly complicit, just like the others on the list.

Unbeknownst to virtually all Americans and people around the world is the fact that in the US the newer and faster HD television and radio technology has a ten-second delay intentionally built into its software. (This is easily confirmed by noting that US national news broadcasts now start at precisely ten seconds past the top of the hour.) This is precisely why this new technology became standard by law and universally mandatory by government edict. This clever software delay was expressly written in by the federal government's Defense Advanced Research Projects Agency (DARPA), which was a founding partner of controlling behemoth tech giant Google.[9]

This deliberately built-in time delay was introduced so that if any theoretically independent television or radio station were to broadcast a world-changing event that the federal government does not want disclosed, like an Apollo astronaut's live confession of the Moon landing fraud, then the CIA can simply cut the transmission before the unfavorable facts are transmitted to the public.

If a President says that their loathing of false information is directed against the news media and not the CIA, then they fail to recognize, or at least acknowledge for reasons of personal safety, that they are *one and the same thing*. As you just read and saw in the previous video, the media *is* controlled by the CIA, whose native language as spies is *lies*. The perhaps *once* honorable Central Intelligence Agency, like many others, first initiated to protect American citizens from foreign adversaries, has been turned against them, like a rabid dog on their owner, spending taxpayer's hard earned money to lie to them without their consent, while simultaneously breaking numerous of their own federal laws in the process, which forbade not only domestic propaganda by the government (until recently when the law was conveniently repealed), it also prohibits lying specifically though the medium of *television*, of which, back in the 1960s and early '70s, the Moon landings were the climax of such illegal televised deception.

The Anti-Propaganda law was specifically enacted as a safeguard for the CIA at its creation in 1947, as the Congress at that time knew full well that the CIA, as a spy agency, would be tempted to repeatedly lie to the public. The No Deception Through Television law was enacted a few years later, because some 1950s television quiz shows gave favorable candidates, whom the public adored, the answers to the questions in advance, so that Americans would be given the candy that they wanted, a staged victory of their fake "heroes". *Time* magazine even once had one such cheating game show winner on the cover of their own magazine, wrongfully calling him "The Smartest Man in America", who only was so because he got the answers to the questions in advance, thusly *cheating* to win, "*for the benefit of the public*". Likewise, just a few years later, the next generation of fake American "heroes", NASA astronauts, would also be featured on *Time* magazine's cover, who also attained their celebrity through cheating, "*for the benefit of the public*".

If "highly respected" *Time* magazine, along with many other *supposedly* "credible" television networks, ran completely false news stories *once*, about the cheating "smartest man in America", either because they themselves were deceived or because they were complicit in the cover up, then it could easily happen again, and it did: Apollo was especially amenable to such deception because unlike events taking place here on Earth, there was absolutely **no independent press coverage** for the alleged lunar missions. The only television images and photographs and other records were supplied in their entirety by the corrupt federal government through its nefarious space and spy agencies.

If a current or future president is *serious* about ethics reform, as they often *claim* they are, then what better rallying cry of the ages than to inform their citizenry that the corrupt and out of control federal government took their hard earned money (about two hundred billion dollars in today's currency) in order to misrepresent the Apollo Moon landing event as seen on TV screens and in the print media worldwide. Surely, this is totally unethical behavior that *requires major reform*. Once every American knows of this outrageous federal government fraud, any President will have an ethics reform mandate unlike any in all of American history, that is, if they are *really* against such corruption, proven only by their exposure of it.

This perpetual misrepresentation of the truth regarding the falsified Moon missions of the Johnson and Nixon administrations must be humbly acknowledged by the *current* leaders of the United States in order for the country to start afresh, otherwise we are just painting over mold that will fatally infest our country's future as well as every citizen thereof. To confess mistakes is noble. This admirable trait is the very reason why President Kennedy had unprecedentedly high approval ratings, specifically because he acknowledged his and his government's mistakes as they happened. He was so beloved by so many Americans and others worldwide, because in carrying out the duties of his office he demonstrated that he was honest above all and humble enough to admit when he was wrong.

The faking of the Apollo Moon landings not only proves the vast intentional and meticulous corruption in the federal government of the United States, which is in dire need of immediate rectification, it also proves that our admired (and hidden) leaders are really a bunch of immature children, afraid of the simple matter of telling the truth that they could not accomplish something they had prematurely boasted about doing. If the truth about this Apollo fraud continues to be swept under the rug again and again, as countless presidential cowards have done before, then America will be forever sealed with the stamp of deception and corruption.

"God opposes the proud, yet gives grace to the humble."

– James 4:6

Chapter Seven
What Constitutes a Conspiracy?

L ife is not so much a battle between right and wrong, as it is a battle between truth and lies, as this generally precedes, and ultimately leads to, good or evil. Truth leads to good. Lies lead to evil. Life is wonderfully simple.

The simple fact is that research suggests that *half* of all crimes are *conspiracies*. Half are done without any forethought, the result of emotional reactions in the heat of the moment. The other half are plotted out in advance, therefore making them conspiracies. Those who would like the public to ignore *half* of all the crimes in the world, by ridiculing those with an intellect to perceive such forethought frauds, are simply those perpetrating the deceptions to begin with.

We have to understand that if a tiny spider, the size of a dime, can meticulously plan and trap its prey weeks in advance, then the human mind, if inclined to evil, can do so much more evil, so much farther in advance. Additionally, a lie, or conspiracy, is the only crime that can exist without tangible evidence. If someone is murdered, there is a dead body. If someone steals, there is the material possession lacking in one place and existing in another. Yet, when someone lies, or plots evil through deception, where is it? A lie is the only crime that you cannot touch, that you cannot see. A lie is purely *ethereal*. This is why lies are the favorite misdeeds of habitual criminals. After all, out of all of the crimes committed in the world for which people are put in prison, so few of them are put there for lying.

The origin of crime is the *lie*, or *conspiracy*, invented in advance of the iniquity, to cover up the wrongdoing before it is even committed. When crimes are committed on a national and international scale, then national and international lies, or conspiracies, are needed to carry them out and conceal them. People, corporations, and governments lie, simply because they are ashamed of what they did or are doing. Lying itself therefore indicates wrongdoing and corruption. Those who lie about their deeds are thereby acknowledging, even to themselves, that what they did or are doing is criminal or unethical, otherwise they would simply tell the truth about what they have done or are doing.

When I was a child, believing in Santa Claus was so much fun. Believing that we live in a magical world where men can fly to the Moon on their very *first* attempt, with antiquated 1960s technology, is fun too, even though, it's worth remembering, the feat cannot be repeated *even with fifty plus years* of better technology, by any nation on Earth, including the one that allegedly achieved it first half a century ago. All truth reminds us that conquering the South Pole, climbing to the peak of Mt. Everest, inventing the first airplane, and the light bulb, were *never, ever* achieved on the *first* attempt, and certainly never *abandoned* once achieved, never to be repeated again as the supposed Moon landings were. All of these points regarding the supposed Moon landings simply defy plain logic, and prove in and of itself that they were falsified, without any fake photography exposed. It is merely people's deep emotional attachment to the event that prevents them from seeing the sad truth.

It is like saying Charles Lindbergh flew across the Atlantic in 1927, yet the feat could not be repeated by any other nation, including the one who made the original claim, half a century later, even though, in reality, during those fifty years, millions of aircraft, one hundred times larger and one million times more advanced, have been flying all over the world on a regular basis. This retardation of human spaceflight, and in fact the backwards track of it **since the alleged Apollo missions**, is completely illogical regarding the perpetual advancement of all sciences and technology, yet this is exactly what we are conditioned to illogically accept, because of media-manipulated "patriotism". There has never been a single instance in the entire history of the world in which a technological advancement was made and then not improved upon, or even *duplicated*, fifty years later... never... ever... except the supposed Moon landings.

These facts alone demonstrate the fraud. The fact is, when you grow up and find out the truth about Santa Claus, you are glad to know it, even if it hurts a little bit, realizing that a painful truth is still better than a sweet lie. The entire world, especially in academia and the aerospace industry, needs to know the painful truth about the fraudulent Moon landings. They will be thankful for it, and it will save the lives of future astronauts, who may wrongfully believe in space travel's ease because of their deception regarding NASA's first attempt to venture beyond Earth.

Why do so many smart people believe this lie? Because they *want* to believe it. Believing such a lie means they can feel that they live in a better world than they actually do. Yet the fact is, they do not. The number one criticism I hear from intelligent, yet disbelieving critics of the Moon landing fraud, is that, *"No one would ever do such a dishonest thing as lying about such an important accomplishment."* Really? They forget that they live in a world full of unthinkable child molestation, vicious murder, hateful racism, deplorable rape, and horrific genocide. In a world such as this, what is it in comparison to merely cheat in a contest, as so many professionals have done before? In these misguided peoples' longing to be part of a society of pride-boosting "miraculous science", *self*-deceived intellectuals fail to grasp the stark and simple fact that **technology does not go backwards**... unless the Moon landings were real.

After Columbus arrived in the New World, within a few years, numerous other European nations traveled to the Americas. After Lewis and Clark ventured to the American west, shortly thereafter, citizens everywhere traveled to the American west. After the Wright brothers accomplished powered flight, within a few years, numerous others repeated their technological accomplishment.

The South Pole has temperatures that reach below 100° Fahrenheit (-73° C) and has hurricane force winds, yet there are bases

there today. Why? Because it is humanly possible. If it were humanly possible to reach the Moon and survive exposure on the
lunar surface, as is supposed to have happened fifty years ago during the Apollo missions, then at the very minimum there should
be at least one crewed base on the Moon *right now.* The fact that
there is not, with half a century of more advancements in rockets
and computational capability, is proof itself that it simply cannot
be done, not even today with fifty more years of advanced technology.[10]

As for the Saturn V rocket, compare its development with that
of the Boeing 747 aircraft, which was built after *seventy years* of
successful aviation history and *millions* of manufactured aircraft,
and was also developed with a *decade* newer technology than that
of the Apollo rocket. Yet the 747 still took one year longer to devel-
op than NASA's alleged Moon landing equipment did, and that
was merely to fly an aircraft seven miles above the ground, which
millions of other aircraft had already done. Even so, the 747 still
had over one hundred and sixty failed engine designs before it
could finally fly! What *magic* equipment the Apollo missions
must have had to have flown thirty-four thousand times higher on
their first attempt! If this equipment worked so well, after an in-
vestment of two hundred billion dollars (present day equivalent),
why aren't they still using this equipment today to regularly fly to
the Moon and back? Instead, NASA deliberately destroyed the
hundreds of billions of dollars worth of hardware to dispose of all
the evidence of their deception.

The problem is, the majority of Americans are not willing to
give up this deep emotional imprinting in order to see the plain-
ness of this harsh and startling reality. When it comes to perceiving the truth in a world full of lies, historically the *majority*
has always been *initially* deceived, and later proved wrong by the
minority of their contemporaries, whom they persecuted and considered deluded at the time, when in fact it was the *majority* who
believed the lies, all the while adamantly thinking they were right
while condemning those who actually spoke the truth.

Does a person know it when they are deceived? No, they do

not. A person can be sincere, and be sincerely wrong.

At one time the *majority* of *scientists* thought that the world was flat. The *majority* of *astronomers* thought that the Earth was at the center of the universe. The *majority* of *physicians* thought that bleeding the sickness out of a person would lead to their cure. The *majority* of Americans thought that Nixon was honest. Likewise, as history repeats itself again and again, a majority of *American* scientists, astronomers, physicians, and citizens think that the Apollo missions were real, yet their titles and majority do not equal truth, as history has well proven, and will prove again.

Why is it so difficult for them to see the truth? Very simple... Pride.

"The Pride of your heart has deceived you."

– Obadiah 1:3

Pride is simply the *un*-willingness to be wrong, just as humility is the *willingness* to be wrong. The great thing about being wrong, which is what I had to finally admit about the lunar fakery, is that I am learning something new, and I am no longer walking through life in error. The bad thing about being right all the time, is that a person cannot learn anything new, and is living in a *self*-deceived state, which is the very worst kind of deception.

When someone else deceives me, if I try hard enough, I can eventually figure it out if I want to. After all, I know that other people cannot be trusted all of the time. Yet when I am *self*-deceived, it is nearly impossible for me to overcome this, because the person I am relying on for facts is *myself*... and of course I can trust myself... even when I am wrong!

Just like a guilty defendant's skilled lawyers in a trial, no matter how plain the condemning evidence is, their manipulative lawyer-like minds have an explanation for why the truth is a lie, and why lies are the truth, otherwise they would be forced to admit their error, which their pride will not allow them to do, and which also blinds them from perceiving the truth. With every item of evidence submitted to them as to why the Moon landings were falsified, no matter how condemning and obvious, there is always a zealous counter explanation from them to throw away the truth and institute a lie in its place, in order for them to keep their dying status quo fantasy alive. Rather than diligently seeking the truth, at the unacceptable cost of being wrong, the majority of people will (because of their blinding pride in the accomplishments of themselves and like-minded others) rather than searching for the truth, instead look for others who agree with what they already falsely believe, so as to further prove themselves right, even though they are wrong.

Again, the real question is, if you had cancer, would you want to know? Or would you rather have your doctor lie to you and tell you that everything was just fine ... even though it really is not? As I already said, sometimes you have to cut off a diseased limb to save your life. The same is true of the beloved lunar landings. A costly admission, yet a saving one as well. Sadly most Americans, due to years of conditioning, are as stubbornly closed minded about the subject as that university professor who said that even a direct Apollo astronaut confession would not convince him of the truth.

The answer to seeing the reality concerning the Moon landings is very simple, yet most people will stubbornly refuse to take even one step in this direction, and instead of merely considering the *possibility* that the missions were staged, these deniers of the facts before their eyes will continue to make excuses, even for the newly-discovered blatant false photography that proves the fraud beyond any doubt to everyone else.

The simple reason why people do not see the truth of this deception is merely because they will not even consider the *possibility* of such a government deception. If you simply open your mind to the *possibility* of this fraud, then your eyes are *instantaneously* opened to the revealing evidence. If you will not even consider the Apollo deception as a *possibility*, then your perception is forever closed to the repeated truth right in front of you. It is that simple. Pride and stubbornness prohibits the perception of the truth, just as open mindedness and humility reveals it. I went from being the greatest fan of the Moon missions to a leading critic thereof, simply because I was willing to be wrong, and favored unpleasant truth more than boastful tradition.

If the Apollo missions were genuine, then they hold a place of prominence in the annals of human history. If they were *not* real, then this *deception* is actually a *more significant moment in history than if they had actually gone!* Thusly, this great truth, that of faking the Moon missions out of pride, arrogance and greed, is being withheld by a minority within the US government agencies. Why? Simply because they want to continue to get way with their ongoing deceptions.

Humanity's character, and especially that of America, will be forever stunted from growth and advancement if the Moon landing deception is continually perpetuated, the very recovery of which would come by simply admitting this fraud with its deplorable dishonesty. Unless we are willing to face and confess the cold hard facts of our errors, much like a disciplined athlete rejecting an appealing yet detrimental candy bar, then we will forever be under the spell, and complete control of, this diabolical hidden minority of government leaders, who represent themselves rather than the people, all the while *asserting the exact opposite.*

The falsified Moon landings are absolute proof that this *is* the state in which America and the world exists today, the very admission of which would lead to these unscrupulous leaders' demise and begin the restoration of America. I maintain this is why that there are more than a hundred websites and films in existence today, specifically dedicated to squashing the emerging truth of the blatant and deplorable falsification of the Apollo missions. The fact is, if the Moon landings were so "obviously" real, as the public are falsely lead to believe, then anyone who says otherwise is an idiot. Why then are there more than a hundred websites and videos, which took tens of thousands of hours to produce, specifically designed to refute the insane ranting of morons? As Shakespeare so famously said, *"Thou does protest too much."* An appropriate quote is from James Mason as Mr. Jordan in *Heaven*

Can Wait: "The likelihood of one individual being right, increases in direct proportion to the intensity with which others are trying to prove him wrong." Even former President Clinton, who once held the (allegedly) highest office in the land, doubts the authenticity of the Moon missions. On page 156 of his autobiography *My Life* he writes:

> Just a month before, Apollo 11 astronauts Buzz Aldrin and Neil Armstrong had left their colleague, Michael Collins, aboard spaceship *Columbia* and 'walked on the moon', beating by five months President Kennedy's goal of putting a man on the moon before the decade was out. The old carpenter asked me if I really believed it happened. I said sure, I saw it on 'television'. He disagreed; he said that he didn't believe it for a minute, that 'them television fellers' could make things look real that weren't. Back then, I thought he was a crank. During my eight years in Washington, I saw some things on TV that made me wonder if he wasn't ahead of his time.[11]

If a President of the United States is publicly expressing his doubts as to the authenticity of the Moon landings (albeit, after he had safely left office), and is calling those who perceive the truth of this event "ahead of their time", shouldn't you also reconsider your thinking about this matter, if you haven't already? Furthermore, if the United States is willing to mislead the entire world and its own citizens about such an historic event, described as "the greatest accomplishment in human history", then what other significant modern events are these corrupt governmental agencies also cleverly staging right now to deceive the public for their own nefarious reasons?

"Apollyon" (the origin of "Apollo")
means "The Devil" or "Deceiver"

– Revelation 9:11

Chapter Eight
Astronauts Gone Wild

Please watch the video *Astronauts Gone Wild* at **Sibrel.com** and click on *Moon Man* link **#6**.

A year after I produced *A Funny Thing Happened...* I suppose influenced by childhood courtroom television programs wherein witnesses take an oath on the Bible as to the truth of their statements, I came up with the idea of tracking down as many Apollo astronauts as I could and simply ask them if they would swear on the Bible as to the authenticity of their alleged Moon missions. It was during the production of this follow-up documentary *Astronauts Gone Wild* that my infamous encounter with Buzz Aldrin occurred, in which he punched me in the face after I called him "A liar, a coward, and a thief."

I certainly did not wake up that morning intending to say those strong words to Aldrin, neither did he set out to punch me in the face that day. It was just one of those spontaneous moments that got heated up, and in my opinion, Aldrin overreacted. Even if he were to have walked on the Moon, it would be hard to call him an American hero when he will not defend the constitutional right of free speech, instead physically attacking anyone who utters words of criticism against him, like so many arrogant dictators have done. A great thing about America is that presidential candidates can openly call each other "liars" when debating the facts, yet they do not punch each other in the face for doing so. If they did, they would not win any election or be idolized by anyone, so why is Aldrin still idolized after violently attacking his critic when anyone else would receive shame for doing the very same thing?

I have received so many emails with these similar words, "I am not a violent person, but I loved seeing you get punched, and I hope it happens again." This is like saying "I am faithful to my spouse, but I flirt with others." (*Matthew 5:27-28*) These *are* violent people who are in self-denial of their love for violence. When someone reacts with violence, or salivates at the sight of it, simply because I say that the lunar landings were fraudulent, then like a radical religious sect which kills people for criticizing their "prophet", this type of violent reaction is irrefutable proof itself that the Apollo missions have become a *god* to them, and a *false god* at that, whose "prophet" I have insulted. The fact that an *alleged* "prophet" of religion, or the supposed Moon landings, has to be perpetually defended, and with violence, is *proof itself* that what is being defended is *false*. Additionally, when it comes to false religion, just as it is with any misrepresented event, it is this very *fanaticism* that not only prevents people from seeing the truth about their over-adored apostatized idol, it is the very thing which proves that they are wrong in the first place!

The more fanatical people become because I point out that their "Moon landing gods" are frauds, the more this same fanatical behavior demonstrates their error on this subject to begin with. I have received uncounted death threats, just for saying to my fellow Americans that their federal government lied to them on at least *one* occasion. Has anyone on the "Truther" side of this argument ever threatened the slightest violence against those who wrongly believe that the Moon landings are real? I can firmly answer "No, not ever." This *fanatical* and often vicious defense of something that is supposed to be so "obvious", is *proof itself* that what is being defended is a *lie*.

The simple truth is, if I *really* had walked on the Moon, and someone thought otherwise, I would find that hysterically funny. If someone asked me to swear on the Bible to that presumed fact, if it indeed was a fact, why in the world would I object to legally affirming such an event if it were genuinely real? Instead, Aldrin reacted to the request as if I had walked up to him in the company of his wife and asked him how his secret mistress was doing! If he *really* had walked on the Moon, my saying otherwise would be like throwing a feather at him. Why would anyone react so violently to someone for throwing a feather at them? If, on the other hand, I were publicly exposing a *real* crime of his *infidelity* against his fellow citizens, one which he had gotten away with for decades and built a lifelong financially beneficial reputation on, then you could certainly see *why* he would react with such violent hatred toward someone exposing his involvement in the Apollo fraud on international television – which is *exactly* how he reacted.

While I do believe that the things I said about Aldrin are true, that he *is* a liar, a coward, and a thief, I now feel that it was inappropriate to rebuke an older man so harshly. Additionally, I too have been a liar, a coward, and a thief, it is just that I am mindful to be repentant of these things and Aldrin has yet to be. If I were to do it all over again, I am not sure that I would have even made my second film *Astronauts Gone Wild* in which I confronted the astronauts, as it even makes me a little uncomfortable to watch it. It is nevertheless, as many supporters my films have noted, a benefit to the historical record when viewed in the future, that these men were given the opportunity to come clean, and they instead adamantly chose to go to their graves with this poisonous lie of theirs.

Because of these after-the-fact revelations of my missteps in making this follow-up documentary to *A Funny Thing Happened...* as I struggle daily to better myself in life's uphill spiritual battle, I later offered Aldrin a sincere apology for my disrespectful words to him, and that very day he very graciously rewarded me by purchasing a DVD of *A Funny Thing Happened...* from my website. Understandably, if people stumble upon *Astronauts Gone Wild* initially on the internet, having never seen my first film on this subject which goes into great detail as to why the deception is indeed a fact, their opinion of the truth about the Apollo missions, as well as my sincere efforts, painstaking diligence, and absolute surety of this truth so as to make this *second* documentary in which I confront these lying men, might be dramatically misunderstood, as this follow-up film does not offer the similar compelling proofs and overviews of the fraud as my first film did.

At the beginning of *Astronauts Gone Wild* I show my first in-

terview with astronaut Buzz Aldrin. This was about a year before
the infamous second interview when he punched me in the face.
His other two crewmembers of the maiden faking-of-the-Moon-
landing trip, have mostly escaped exposure, as they refuse almost
all media requests for interviews, being only seen on anniversary
commemorations every five or ten years (I think that's because
they have a differently oriented moral compass than Aldrin and
prefer not to perpetually lie about such a scandalous event). Buzz
Aldrin, on the other hand, loves the limelight and cashing in on
his misappropriated notoriety. Aldrin has sold numerous books
about his fake Moon experiences, is always the person that talk
shows call first when they want to hear from a "moonwalker",
and every few years he pulls out some "newly-discovered memen-
tos" from his mission (like quarters which he claims were on the
Moon with him) which he endlessly sells at auctions for hundreds
of thousands of dollars, which in and of itself is an additional
criminal fraud.

It was at one of Aldrin's book signings that I arranged this
first interview with him, held privately in the bookstore manager's office afterwards. Unbeknownst to Aldrin, in attendance with
me were some reputable federal government employees, who were
well aware of the fraud and were there to observe his rebuttal of
what was about to happen. I had two large professional television
cameras there, several lights, and a high quality wireless microphone attached to Aldrin, who thought that the purpose of the
interview was to promote his book, although this was wrongly
assumed on his part, as I had never said as such. I had also set up
a large television monitor, for the purpose of showing Aldrin the
newly discovered outtakes of fake photography from his mission,
which he personally filmed and would therefore undoubtedly remember.

As I showed Aldrin the revealing footage of fake photography
from his flight which proves that he never left low-Earth orbit on
the TV monitor, everyone present could see him begin to squirm.
"How did you get this footage?" he inquired. "Serendipity" I replied. Because my television production company at that time was

named "ABCDigital" (so that I could appear first in the Yellow Pages), he had apparently wrongly assumed that I was with the major news network "ABC". This additional serendipity worked to my advantage, as with two broadcast cameras and film lighting there, belonging as he believed to "ABC *News*", Aldrin thought that the story of his historic fraud had, *at that very moment*, broken worldwide! It was then, in his anger, that he exclaimed, "And this makes you a real famous person that has discovered this and reveals all this stuff! What an ego you must have to want to propel yourself like this!"

The question then arises, if I was wrong about my discovery, then how could I become a famous person or advance my career by exposing nothing?

Therefore, this statement *itself* from Aldrin is a *direct admission of his guilt in the matter*, as he didn't say I was *wrong* about my discovery, rather he said that I had *impure motives* for revealing this important truth to the world.

In his startled, befuddled, and angry state, Aldrin went on to utter another unplanned admission of his guilt, "Well you're talking to the wrong guy! Why don't you talk to the administrator of NASA? We're passengers! We're guys going on a flight!"

As Aldrin admitted that the entire Apollo 11 crew were only *"passengers"*, then this certainly means that no one ever *piloted* the LM to the lunar surface, as previously claimed, because a *passenger* and a *pilot* are certainly two very different things.

Aldrin then fiddled in his briefcase for an extended period of time, stalling while he composed himself and tried to figure out what to do next. He then asked for my business card. It was at this point that he realized that the person who had just caught him in his life of fraud was with ABC*Digital*, a private television production company, rather than ABC *News* as he had feared, which led him into making the *two* previous admissions of guilt. As it dawned on Aldrin that he had gravely misspoken by admitting his guilt in the Apollo fraud *twice*, he started to backpedal on his confession and tried to reassert, though not very convincingly, his mission's alleged authenticity. When Aldrin realized that he had made these *two* admissions of guilt on camera, he then threatened to sue me if I showed these guilt-revealing remarks of his to anyone. Certainly, if these two statements were *not* admissions of guilt, then he would have no problem sharing these recorded statements with the public and would not have to threaten legal action to prevent their release.

Next up in *Astronauts Gone Wild* I interviewed Apollo 12 astronaut Alan Bean, who then made a living, not by repeatedly pulling endless souvenirs out of his closet for hundred-thousand-dollar auctions which he claimed were with him on the Moon, but rather by selling paintings falsely depicting him on the lunar surface, for the same auctions. (If he were not known for this deceitful claim of his, each painting would likely be worth only hundreds of dollars.) I conducted this interview in Bean's home. I had contacted him and explained that I was a filmmaker producing a documentary about the Apollo missions, which was true. He just wrongly assumed that I believed that the missions were real and that my film would perpetuate that grotesque lie. Notable revelations in his interview were that the lunar module, somehow, "miraculously" powered air-conditioning for three days nonstop, combatting an outside temperature of some 250° Fahrenheit (121° C), with what were essentially a bunch of car batteries. As I have already said, my astute executive producer laughed out loud at this mathematically and electrically impossible claim. Bean also said that the descent engine to the lunar surface was *completely quiet* because of the "vacuum of space" (a catch-all excuse for numerous inconsistent claims which expose the fraud), yet another Apollo astronaut, Eugene Cernan, said that the descent engine was "very loud."

Indeed the LM was a "miraculous" flying machine, in that it was full of incapable fantasies. On its twenty-second testing in May 1968, it nearly killed Neil Armstrong during a simulated lunar landing at Ellington Air Force Base. Propellant and instrumentation issues led to Armstrong losing control and ejecting less than one second before the LM simulator crashed and burst into flames, and all this was at some 200ft above the ground. It took six months to sort those problems out. Then just another nine months later, the LM would *allegedly* be working flawlessly in the dangerous untested environment of the Moon for the Apollo 11 mission, and for every time thereafter.

The next important discovery in Bean's testimony is him revealing, albeit accidentally, that the Apollo crews never went though the vast deadly radiation belts that surround Earth.

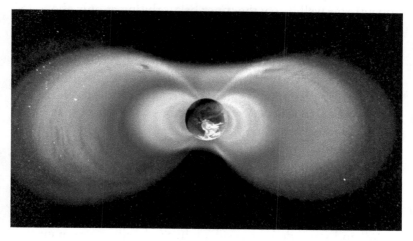

Cross section of the Van Allen belts, CGI simulation for December 2003, NASA/ Goddard Space Flight Center. The Van Allen belts surround the Earth while leaving gaps centered around the north and south magnetic poles, these Van Allen belts generally consist of two toroidal rings of energetic charged particles. Solar wind activity has been found to generate temporary belts within this region. Note that Apollo did not exit via the polar regions. The distance from Earth of these two belts is generally described as multiples of the Earth's radius (one Earth radius is 3963 miles) and written as Earth Radii (R_E) distances added in statute miles. NASA's depiction of the activity in the belts only shows the belts to a distance of 8 radii from the surface of Earth, rather than the minimum of 10 radii they actually occupy.

The inner belt can vary from some 124 miles above the Earth (the South Atlantic anomaly) but is generally said to start at some 620 miles altitude, with a very intense region 1.5 R_E (Earth Radii) off the surface of the Earth, around 5,944 miles, and then the belt carries on through to 2 R_E or 7,926 miles. After a small gap the outer belt begins some 3 R_E or 11,889 miles out, its region of

greatest intensity lies between 4 to 5 R_E out. That is 15,852 miles
through to 19,815 miles. And after that, the outer belt continues
on to some 10 R_E 39,630 miles.[12]
    These belts are far more complex and lethal than was known
at the time of Apollo and these dimensions can fluctuate, as can
their deadly particle populations. This dangerous unpredictability
is exactly why the International Space Station and all current astronauts stay well below the inner belt (orbiting at only about 250
miles above the Earth), and why only the long-ago "Moon astronauts" are the only ones who have *claimed* to have go through this
deadly region of space, and that with untried 1960s technology!
This is precisely why orbiting the Earth at a height of a mere two
hundred and fifty miles is *still* the preferred limit for astronaut
crews today, *even with current more advanced technology*, specifically
due to the aforementioned lethal space radiation that begins at
higher altitudes, which I will discuss later in greater detail.
    At first Bean said, "I'm not sure we went far enough out to
encounter the Van Allen radiation belt. Maybe we did." Thereby,
perhaps unwittingly, revealing that the Apollo astronauts *actually*
never left low-Earth orbit.
    When I reminded the accidentally truth-telling astronaut that
he would first have to go through some thirty-nine thousand miles
of intense radiation belts in order to reach the Moon he said, "**Oh
yeah. Then I guess we went right through them.**" I then asked
Bean if the radiation caused any strange phenomena, to which
he said "no". When I pointed out to him that during the highest
altitude *ever* flown by a Space Shuttle crew (Discovery STS-82 in
February 1997) they reported seeing radiation-causing "shooting
stars" when they closed their eyes, because the radiation was so
intense, Bean then claimed to have seen the same phenomenon
on his 1969 flight. When I pointed out to him that I believed that
this 1997 shuttle mission was the very *first* astronaut crew to ever
report this strange phenomenon, twenty-four years *after* his 1969
mission, he then changed his story again and said "Not on our
mission, as they hadn't been discovered yet." He then went on to
later forget this very statement that he had just made and changed

his story *yet again*, to say that he *did* see the same radiation effect on his 1969 mission!

Because Alan Bean was willing to lie while swearing on a Bible, I asked him if he believed in a Divine Creator, to which he replied "pretty much" (whatever that means), as he was one of the few Apollo astronauts who dared to swear on the Bible that they actually walked on the Moon (the other two who did so were already avowed atheists). When I asked Bean to swear on the Bible with the understanding that if he lied about the authenticity of his supposed Moon mission he would be guilty of *treason*, he somehow took offence to this, and defended his duplicitous actions by saying that, if he did lie about the missions, that it would not be treason, as "treason is when you sell out your country". Which was again, a very significant and interesting statement. Apparently, as a former member of the military, he was sensitive to the accusation of "treason", justifying the Moon landing fraud to himself as being, somehow, a patriotic endeavor. He disagreed with me that deceiving his fellow citizens about the Moon landings, in an operation that cost the 2002 equivalent of one hundred and thirty-five billion dollars (now an equivalent of two hundred billion dollars) was not selling out his country. I think it clearly is. Finally, he just cursed at me and threw me out of his house... after I had paid him his insisted upon $2000 an hour, *in cash*, for the privilege of being lied to.

Up next was Apollo 10 and 16 astronaut John Young, who I met in Los Angeles at a conference on space travel. In that remarkable, unedited footage of the Apollo 11 outtakes of a fake space scene, the astronauts specifically refer to Young's preceding Apollo mission, in which he *claimed* to have orbited the Moon without lading, which is also a lie. While the Apollo 11 crew concocted their fake filming of pretending to be halfway to the Moon, Neil Armstrong says, "This is the way 'Ten' did it". CapCom Charlie Duke's comments were from Goldstone who said that "they see no white spots as we saw on [Apollo] 10. Looks like the AGC's working real well... The f/22 looks good. Over." This means that Young, as well as *all* the other Apollo astronauts, also never left

Earth orbit. (In order to stage for the public a "progress report" on Kennedy's misspoken goal, Apollo 10 falsely claimed to have practiced the descent into lunar orbit without actually landing). When I pointed out the discovery of this revealing fake photography of Apollo 11 to John Young of Apollo 10, in which they specifically refer to *him* doing the exact same photographic deception on *his* mission, Young turned pale white, tried to cover his alarm with a fake smile, threatened to hit me, and then literally ran away from the interview in fear. When people see all of this in *Astronauts Gone Wild*, they are truly stunned by Young's frightened reaction at the discovery of this revealing Apollo 11 footage, proving yet again, that something is *very wrong* with the supposed Apollo missions.

I interviewed Eugene Cernan next. As Neil Armstrong was falsely proclaimed to have been the first man on the Moon, Cernan was falsely proclaimed to be the last. As such, more than the other Apollo astronauts on the previous missions, Cernan had the benefit of additional training in the art of lying about these fake missions of theirs. I have taken about two hundred hours of acting classes myself, have been in live theatre productions over five hundred times, and have taught acting classes about one hundred times. In my opinion, this man had professional acting training. I could tell from his body language and his technique of story telling. Why would he need theatrical training to talk about his Moon missions if he had *really* been there? Unlike the others, Cernan had been taught to visualize the false scenes he was describing, in order to add to their believability. This is why he was later selected to be a live television commentator during some of the other NASA missions. Nevertheless, despite Cernan's calm *appearance*, his underarms sweated profusely when I interviewed him about his lies, severely staining his shirt, plus he snapped at his dogs repeatedly as the interview became ever more challenging, revealing that his *perceived* "calmness" was really *an act*.

It was in Cernan's interview, filmed at his home, that he stated that the descent engine to the Moon was "very loud", all the while forgetful that Apollo 12's Alan Bean had said that he could not hear the descent engine at all "because of the vacuum of space" (their repeated catch-all excuse for unexplainable inconsistencies). Furthermore, during Cernan's alleged "loud engine" decent, as he transmitted conversations of what he was supposedly doing while he was allegedly landing on the Moon, he forgot that no sound at all was actually heard in the background. This was because Cernan was really just reading a prepared script from the quiet solitude of Earth orbit, all the while the television networks showed rudimentary NASA animation *simulating* the supposed landing, that they claimed could not be shown live, though it easily could have, *if* they were really there.

In fact, no *live video* of any of the landings was ever shown on television, only pre-created animated *simulations*. In my opinion, this was simply because they had not figured out how to fake these alleged landings convincingly. If they were *really* landing on the Moon, and brought various television cameras with them on board, as claimed, then all they would have to do is point one of these cameras out the window during the landings (or during the entire flight to the Moon), or simply mount one of these cameras to the side of the spacecraft pointing downwards, in order to show the landings as they took place, none of which they did, simply because *they were not there*. As it was with all of the Moon mission *presentations*, it was the blind *trust* of the public, who took everything they were shown by their government to be truthful, which made this deception so very easy, probably easier than the perpetrators first imagined. Added to this ease of swallowing this lie, was the public's *desire to believe* that they were great enough to land on the Moon.

Another one of Cernan's mistakes was that he claimed that the Earth was continually visible just over the lunar horizon during his entire moonwalk (not much higher in the sky as the photo from the Apollo 17 missions actually shows) and that the Earth was four times bigger than a full Moon on Earth. Why is it then, that there is not even **one** photograph of this amazing sight; a picture of Cernan (or any astronaut, on *any* mission) standing on the Moon with the large Earth right over his shoulder? Surely, if you were *really* on the Moon, and the Earth was *really* right over the horizon the entire time as Cernan claimed, you would want a picture of yourself standing there with the big Earth right behind you, like a tourist in Paris with the Eiffel Tower behind them. Yet the only photograph of the Earth allegedly taken from the lunar surface during his or any mission, shows it far up in the sky, and looking slightly smaller than a full Moon as seen from Earth. Please see **Sibrel.com** *Moon Man* link #7.

Cernan was right when he said that the Earth is four times larger than the Moon (albeit he was rounding up: on average the disk of the Earth is 3.66 times larger in diameter) but he was misleading by implying an earthrise. We all know that the reason that the Moon looks huge when we see it rising on our horizon is because the atmosphere is distorting its actual disk diameter. Here is the reason why there could never be an image of the Earth looming behind an astronaut, even when we finally manage that feat: according to Mark Robinson of Arizona State University in Tempe, principal investigator for LROC:

> From the Earth, the daily moonrise and moonset are always inspiring moments, however, lunar astronauts will see something very different: viewed from the lunar surface, the Earth never rises or sets. Since the moon is tidally locked, *Earth is always in the same spot above the horizon*, varying only a small amount with the slight wobble of the moon.[13] [emphasis added]

So it would be an impossibility to see what he claimed to see from the lunar surface, and even NASA states that the only way to get an 'earthrise image' is *by arranging the orbit of a spacecraft so as to artificially create it* – and when they posted an 'earthrise' image on October 12, 2015 that is exactly what they did, in all respects. Even though this image was taken one the day *before* the full Earth, we see a *completely* illuminated disk that would not occur until the evening of October 13th.

Cernan went on to claim that seeing the Earth from the lunar surface was a "comfort" to him. I would think that it would be a frightening sight to view your home planet from a distance of 247,083 miles away, knowing that you had a hazardous and uncertain trip ahead of you, with no rescue available should either the LM's small single engines fail to get you up off of the Moon's surface to rendezvous with the orbiting, and life saving, Command Module for any reason. Even if that link up went according to plan, the CSM still had to traverse all those thousands of miles and then re-enter the atmosphere successfully deploying a *skip re-entry* no US craft has ever achieved to date.

You can tell from watching Cernan's interview that as soon as I mentioned the deadly Van Allen radiation belts, which he would have to pass through to reach the Moon, he immediately became concerned about the direction of the interview. At that very moment his body language suddenly changed. Shifting into a defensive posture, he folded his arms while simultaneously becoming irritable to the point of repeatedly yelling at his dogs, unwittingly revealing through these actions that I had touched on a well-known contradictory point, after which he was reluctant to talk about the radiation obstacle any longer. When I persisted in this line of questioning, because the radiation issue is so highly relevant to astronauts' inability to leave low-Earth orbit, even to this day, the well-trained spokesman nevertheless lost his stamina and became confused as to how to best reply, thereafter losing his train of thought. All of this forced Cernan to quickly assert that "We *weren't* passengers". Interestingly, this comment had nothing to do with the Van Allen belt controversy we were discussing, yet was genuinely remarkable, in that 'passengers' is *precisely* how Aldrin had described the Apollo 11 astronauts when justifying his misconduct, by blaming NASA leadership for the fraud instead of admitting his own responsibility in the deception. The fact that Cernan chose the exact same expression that Aldrin had used when they were both experiencing challenging interviews about their lifetime of lying, denotes some kind of conditioned response these men had been trained to say - or programed to use - when being exposed for their fraudulent actions.

When I read out to Cernan the Apollo rocket designer's original statement that it was *mathematically impossible* to fly to the Moon in a single rocket, as Cernan had claimed he had done, rather that *three* rockets would be needed and that each rocket would have to weigh *three hundred and twenty times* more than the Apollo rocket did, Cernan again crossed his arms defensively and then put an end to the interview. I still managed to ask him how the genius rocket designer, Wernher von Braun, could recant his original math by *thirty-two thousand percent* in order to reach Kennedy's naïve impossible goal, to which Cernan had no reply. As Cernan had just sternly defended the authenticity of his fake mission for the entire interview, he too, like Alan Bean, then felt obligated to swear on the Bible in order to reinforce his previous false statements.

As a postscript on Cernan's interview; at one point he had claimed that he "doesn't give a damn" about people who say that the Moon landings were falsified, yet he later contradicted his alleged lack of interest by privately admitting to me that he had a copy of Bill Kaysing's book exposing his deception, in order to keep up with the developing investigation into his fraud. Though not shown in *Astronauts Gone Wild*, I also offered Cernan a ten thousand dollar deposit to borrow his "lunar dust" sample in his living room, in order to take it to a laboratory to authenticate, to which he adamantly refused. This was because it was probably just firewood ash.

In the next part of *Astronauts Gone Wild* I caught up with Apollo 11 astronaut Michael Collins of the first claimed mission, who like Neil Armstrong did not give interviews other than special anniversary appearances. Interesting, isn't it? Two of the three men who participated in "the greatest event in the history of the world" do not ever want to talk about it, quite unlike genuine winning athletes of the Super Bowl, who most gladly and proudly give numerous and repeated interviews about their great *and genuine* accomplishment.

At the executive producer's request, at this point in *Astronauts Gone Wild* I first edited in a brief clip from *A Funny Thing Happened...* that of the Apollo 11 crew's only formal and complete press conference of their alleged historical mission. You can see from the press conference picture below (*left to right*) that Buzz Aldrin, Neil Armstrong, and Michael Collins look as though they are obliged to do something that they find morally reprehensible, which was *precisely* the case. As this incredible fraud was indeed taking place, it was a soul-souring experience that could not be wiped away from their faces. This is exactly why their expressions for nearly the entire press conference looked like they were attending their mother's funeral, rather than being the winners of a great victory. The same was true the day of their launch. Instead of joking as they were about to risk life and limb in an untried mission, as was always done before *genuine* space missions to ease the tension, they were all uncharacteristically solemn and melancholy, to the astonishment of the uninformed assistants around them.

Victory or Defeat? Apollo 11 Post Flight Press Conference (July 1969).

At this one-time event, a journalist, Patrick Moore (a well-known British astronomer) asked the astronauts if they saw any stars from the lunar surface. Even though these three men were supposed to be the only ones in existence who had such a unique one-of-a-kind experience, they were nevertheless aided in describing their mission by a teleprompter, hidden in their desk, which directed them what to say about the event. (In the picture above the teleprompter can be seen in front of Neil Armstrong's right hand holding the pen.) When Moore asked whether or not they saw the beautiful stars of the universe from the surface of the Moon, Neil Armstrong replied, "We were never able to see stars from the lunar surface or on the daylight side of the moon by eye without looking through the optics. I don't recall during the period of time that we were photographing the solar corona what stars we could see." – Really? He was on the Moon for the very first time in mankind's existence looking out into the vastness of space and "didn't recall" if he saw the beautiful stars of the universe, more clearly than ever before, in the vast expanse of the pitch black atmosphere-free sky?

To this noticeably awkward moment, Aldrin reacted with a flinch, uneasy by Armstrong's odd reply. Fellow crewmember Michael Collins then tried to help out by reminding them of their rehearsed answer to this question, should it be asked, by replying, "I don't remember seeing any." The problem with Collins' answer is that in attempting to correct Armstrong's fumble, Collins created one of his own. He was *supposed* to have been orbiting the Moon while the other two were *allegedly* walking on the surface, thusly he was not in a position to even see stars from the lunar surface. Lightning then struck twice in the very same place, because if you get a written transcript of the press conference (as this was the only public record of it at the time, with no internet, and no videos), NASA later corrected Collins' mistake and attributed his reply of "I don't remember seeing any" to *Aldrin* instead, who was supposed to be on the lunar surface, not *Collins*.

Why would they need to *deliberately lie* in the written record of the historical transcript of who answered the "stars" question if they *really* went to the Moon?

The executive producer of my two films on this subject thought that this was highly significant, and this is why he asked that I show this mistake of Collins at this point in the film.

I caught up with Collins as he traveled to the store from his

home on the weekend. As he, like Armstrong, didn't give interviews, my executive producer hired a notable private detective
agency to track down the addresses of these reluctant astronauts.
The cameraman and I flew to his hometown, rented a large sedan,
and parked outside of his residence early on a Saturday morning. I figured that, it being the weekend, Collins would eventually
leave home to run an errand. He did so after about three hours of
waiting. The cameraman and I followed Collins to a local market
and I approached him there in the parking lot with my camera
crew. I asked Collins about the newly-discovered footage of fake
photography from his mission. Instead of replying to real evidence
of the fraud, which he was highly familiar with, as he was there
when the fake Earth model was being filmed, Collins' trained
standard reply kicked in. He ignored the evidence, and using his
programed juvenile defense, labeled me as "wacko" for knowing
the hidden truth. Very sad, isn't it? If you believe lies, then you are
called "normal", and if you see the truth, then you are labeled as
"crazy" by the rest of society, who are *actually* the ones who are
"insanely" deceived. Collins also refused to swear on the Bible
that he left Earth orbit to circle the Moon as he has falsely claimed
his entire life, and acted like a "wacko" himself when he walked
up to our camera and pressed his nose against the lens before
angrily departing.

   Up next in *Astronauts Gone Wild* was Alfred Worden from
Apollo 15. His false story, like Collins, is that he orbited the
Moon while his fellow crewmembers walked on the surface, prov-
en impossible by the lethal space radiation as previously discussed.
I caught up with Worden at NASA in Florida during a public relations campaign of theirs. He too, like Collins, would not swear on
the Bible that he orbited the Moon, and also like Collins, offered
the same standard trained reply, that it was "nonsense" to recognize and acknowledge government deception.

   At the same NASA event as Worden, I found Apollo 8 astronaut William Anders, who also falsely claimed that he had orbited
the Moon. He too would not swear on the Bible that his mission's claims were authentic. Soon after my brief encounter with

him, NASA security removed us from the facility and threatened us with arrest, simply for asking a challenging question, despite having a scheduled appointment to do so and their own media credentials authorizing us to be there, specifically to ask journalistic questions of Apollo astronauts. At the time I felt like I was in North Korea or China, places where journalists are only welcomed if they cooperate with government officials and ask preapproved easy questions, and are then harassed and threatened with arrest, just like we were, if they fail to cooperate, all for simply asking a question about government corruption. Here in America, when a reporter at NASA makes a challenging inquiry about the agency's actions, security forces likewise quickly remove them and threaten them with arrest. Again, is there *really* a "free" press in America, or is that concept, like the supposed Moon landings, also an *illusion*?

The next Apollo astronaut encounter in *Astronauts Gone Wild* includes the infamous punch by Buzz Aldrin. On this second recorded occasion with Aldrin (like Armstrong, there were a few private conversations not recorded) I was a surprise guest of a Japanese television production company which had scheduled an interview with Aldrin at a hotel near his residence in Beverly Hills, California. I had worked with these Japanese filmmakers in the recent past for a television special in their country which questioned the authenticity of the Moon landings, a truth easier to explore with an open mind over there, because it is outside of the United States' direct propaganda control, and this deception is not repeatedly seared into the conscience of their citizenry regularly since birth. In fact, while about twenty-five percent of Americans now question the validity of the long ago alleged Moon landings (a figure often deliberately misquoted in television programs attempting to squelch the emerging fraud by referencing a two decades older survey with lower numbers), up to three quarters of the rest of the world already recognizes the deception, the specific fraud of which is even taught as curriculum in thousands of foreign universities.[14]

On this second occasion with Aldrin I decided to have my

own crew there alongside the Japanese film crew, so that I would have my own rights to the subsequent footage. When Aldrin again asked for my business card at the beginning of the encounter, I told him that I would give him two, one for him and one for his attorney, as he had previously threatened to sue me if I showed his two recorded admissions of guilt to anyone. Aldrin then went on to accuse me, once again, of being an attention seeker, the very thing that he is supremely guilty of, as he has cashed in on his ill-claimed celebrity more than any other Apollo astronaut, even charging two thousand dollars an hour on this occasion for his lying interview, the very reason why I would later call him "a thief", for taking money to expound on something which he actually did not do.

Next I asked Aldrin, "Do you think you can get to heaven without repenting?" I asked him this question because he had told me, in a previous extended private conversation, that he believed in God. I then said that if his belief was genuine then continuing to lie about his Moon mission was not repentance at all, and that he needed to confess the truth to the world in order to be right with God. (I believe that Aldrin, in the process of lying about the missions, feared swearing on the Bible more than the others because of his private acknowledgment to me of his belief in a Divine Creator.)

Aldrin was with the daughter of his then (now divorced) wife. She attempted to block the lens of our camera while we were filming. I was not aware of this at the time, and this is why my clever cinematographer took the camera off of his shoulder and held it by his side, to make it appear as if he was not filming, though he really continued to do so. Noticing this camera relocating, yet not knowing why, I instructed the cinematographer to resume his normal filming, and he subsequently put the camera back on his shoulder. It was at this point that Aldrin accused me, for the third time, of investigating his fraudulent actions for reasons of personal publicity. I then remind him that it was he who just gave an interview for publicity and for financial gain about something that he did not do. As the conversation became more heated, I called him "a liar, a coward, and a thief"; a *liar* for obvious reasons, a *coward* for endlessly perpetuating this lie for fear of his reputation loss should the truth come out, and a *thief* for continually taking money to share his falsified experiences of a moonwalk that never actually happened. I think it was the "coward" remark that provoked his pride so severely that he punched me in response.

One *hundred percent* of the CIA's mainstream media supported Aldrin for assaulting someone after they expressed their right of freedom of speech in uttering a critical opinion of him. Lies were even fabricated to justify Aldrin's obvious violent lawlessness, and for not being prosecuted for it as the average citizen would be, in order to deny such a blatant inequality in justice. The media lied and said that I had him "backed up against a wall", when the video clearly shows that he was not up against a wall, rather it was I who was backed up against a billboard. The media lied again and said that I "poked him with a Bible", which the video also clearly shows never happened, nor would I have ever done such a thing. The media lied a third time by saying that the reason that he was not arrested for obvious assault was that he was "provoked" by my criticism and *had to* punch me in the face in order to "defend himself" against my *words*, despite the elementary teaching since childhood of *"sticks and stones will break my bones, but names will never hurt me."* Why would the media have to *lie three times* if Aldrin was in the right?

The fact is, the district attorney told me privately, that the reason why they did not prosecute Aldrin for obvious (and video-recorded) assault, was not because they thought that he was "provoked with words", rather because "We are not going to prosecute a national hero." Aldrin is, and always will be, fully protected by the US State. Sadly "justice for all" does not in any way *actually* apply to all, as our own government officials plainly admitted to me was the case. It seems that being a "protected" corrupt member of the United States federal government comes with the right to openly break the law. Had I punched him after he called me "a liar, a coward, and a thief," you can be sure that I would have immediately been arrested and sent to jail. This is further proof that the Apollo Moon walkers have become false gods, and that it is this same blinding radical zealousness which prevents people from seeing the truth about their highly fraudulent actions. It continues to amaze me that people believe lies as the truth, and say that the truth is a lie. What a world.

The next to the last Apollo astronaut that I interviewed in my film *Astronauts Gone Wild* was Neil Armstrong, who was the most difficult of them all to track down. As an investigative journalist, I had already uncovered where he lived years earlier, even before the executive producer hired private detectives to locate all of the other reluctant Apollo astronauts. Armstrong's residence was so concealed from the public record that his own next-door neighbors and mail carrier did not even know that he lived there. At first, I did the same thing as I had done with Collins. I rented a car and parked nearby his home in order to follow him to a public place where I could quickly ask him a few questions in the company of a professional cameraman to record the interview.

The first time I attempted this, when Armstrong arrived at a nearby restaurant, he simply stayed in his car with the windows rolled up, u-turned, and went back home. He then telephoned the police to ask them to command us to leave. When the local police showed up adjacent to our car parked nearby his home, I showed them my media credentials and asserted my journalistic right to follow a public figure in public places. They immediately checked with their local judge, who agreed with me, and who then instructed the police not to interfere with a journalist. After this, I saw the same police officer as before attempting to get around the Judge's order by first privately conferring with Armstrong at his front door and then going over to Armstrong's next-door neighbor, to arrange for them to commit the law violation in the policeman's place, out of misled patriotism no doubt. Apparently they had worked out a scheme for Armstrong's neighbor (who had just found out that Neil Armstrong lived right next door to them) to drive his car between Armstrong's car and mine, to then slow down, and subsequently let Armstrong get away from my interview. This attempt failed, even after the neighbor rammed our car with his and drove us off the road into a yard, as I was able to quickly get back on the road behind Armstrong.

Keep in mind, all of this was done merely to prevent the man, known widely as "the first man on the Moon", from simply answering a few questions from a reporter about his historic mission, about which the public should have a right to know, even if he did go. On Armstrong's third attempt to avoid talking to a reporter, even for half a minute in a parking lot as he entered a restaurant to go to dinner, the same police officer, after the scheme with Armstrong's neighbor had just failed, illegally got in front of our car, put on his brakes and emergency lights, and prevented us from going any further. When I reported this illegal action to the local judge, it was acknowledged by them that what the policeman did was a violation of the law and then they assured me that the officer would be reprimanded, which to my knowledge never happened.

Sad, isn't it? This naïve and deceived police officer and Armstrong's neighbor actually thought that they were aiding an honorable man, when in my opinion, they were in fact helping to protect the leading individual in the Apollo fraud, all the while Neil Armstrong probably smiled and laughed to himself that he had gotten two misguided souls to aid him in his unscrupulous behavior.

On the twenty-fifth anniversary of the notorious first lunar hoax event, about twenty-five years ago and ten years before this encounter of mine with Armstrong, while Armstrong was speaking for just thirty seconds in the White House, Neil Armstrong held back tears as he strongly hinted at the Moon landing deception, when he said that there are "Breakthroughs available to those who can remove one of truth's protective layers." At the time of this very odd statement of Armstrong's, I could see tear-filled compassion in his eyes. Years after this cryptic revealing statement, on two or three separate occasions (some off the record) when I met with Armstrong, that glint of humanity in his eyes was completely gone, succumbed to a seared conscious from decades of lying, after an extended period of time of which, his eyes had turned into soulless ones, just like those of the CIA agents who had followed me from church that faithful day.

About six months after the cameraman and I had been maliciously run off the road by Armstrong's misguided neighbor, the same cameramen found out that Neil Armstrong was making a retirement statement at a bomb making company where he was a token CEO. It was there that I recorded my encounter with him as showcased in *Astronauts Gone Wild*. Armstrong, like most of the other Apollo astronauts, would not take an oath that he was telling the truth about his mission, just as George Bush Junior and Dick Cheney refused to take an oath prior to answering questions about their involvement in 9/11, for fear that they could be prosecuted later for perjury. I even offered Armstrong five thousand dollars in cash to give to his favorite charity (a thousand dollars a second) if he would merely swear to something that is supposed to be so very obvious, yet he adamantly refused to do so, began to shake nervously, and concluded by saying, "Mr. Sibrel, you do not deserve answers."

I should have replied, "So you admit that there *are* answers!" or "If the lead investigative journalist or the Congress and the Senate do not "deserve answers" (as they too were kept in the dark about the fraud) then who exactly is worthy of answers?" I have seen this before, from supremely guilty, yet smart-mouthed men, who answer flippantly when confronted with their unprosecuted crimes. Shortly after I filmed this segment, the company's security team rather violently escorted my cameraman and I out of the building, bruising me for several months thereafter.

I conversed with Armstrong privately on another occasion, in which I pleaded with him, for his own soul's sake, to come clean with the truth before his death. I cannot tell you exactly what his reply was for reasons of confidentiality, yet he made it clear to me that my assessment of the Moon landings is correct, that he appreciated my sincerity, and that he had his own plan for eventual disclosure. Armstrong is said to have died shortly thereafter.

The last Apollo astronaut whom I interviewed in *Astronauts Gone Wild* was Edgar Mitchell of Apollo 14. He too, like Aldrin, Bean, and Cernan, charged two thousand dollars an hour for the privilege of perpetuating the Apollo fraud to an audience. Not only did he have an unfounded reputation for walking on the Moon when he did not, he was also mistakenly known as a "peace guru", to which in my experience, he would reveal himself to be everything but that. Also like Bean and Cernan, he too thought that my interview, conducted in his home, was to glorify him and the corrupt Apollo missions, and to his surprise, the interview instead unfolded into the exact opposite.

In Mitchell's case, like Aldrin's, a television and video player was nearby to show him the newly-discovered footage of fake Apollo photography. Interestingly though, I first asked Mitchell to put in his own reel of footage from his mission, so that it could be playing to the side on the television as I conducted the, mostly harmless, first part of the interview. To my surprise, Mitchell instructed us to just play the tape that was already in there, which he mistakenly believed was a NASA promotional film about his mission, already cued up for the occasion. Instead of playing a NASA Apollo 14 reel which would glorify his lie, Mitchell had accidently left in his VCR a very recent release of a film made by another filmmaker, which also exposed the fact that the scenes which NASA claims were filmed on the Moon in sunlight, were *actually* photographed inside a film studio lit with *electrical* light!

Obviously Mitchell had been keeping up with the recently unfolding revelations of the Apollo deception, but when I asked him what the critical scene being shown on his television meant, one that pointed out the lighting direction discrepancies with various arrows, he smiled nervously, avoided the question, and tried to make it look like the film was about fellow astronaut Aldrin. I again referred to the distinct images on the screen, which clearly questioned the authenticity of the Moon missions, to which Mitchell said that he did not know what the film in his VCR was about. When I persisted with my line of questioning concerning the movie playing on the screen beside him, and it became too apparent what the video was really about *exposing* the Apollo fraud, Mitchell changed his story yet again, to admitting that the film that he accidentally showed really was about the Apollo missions being fabricated.

As Eugene Cernan was the best liar among the group (though still highly flawed), Edgar Mitchell was by far the worst liar of them all. His mistake of cueing up his own copy of a recent film exposing the Apollo deception only made his downfall that much worse. I asked him where he got a copy of this film. He said that he did not remember, and then later, changed this to saying that a random person had sent it to him. When Mitchell uncomfortably and unconvincingly defended himself with the remark, "We did exactly what we said we did," he couldn't even look me in the eye all the way through saying this blatant lie.

I then took out the other Apollo fraud investigator's videotape from his VCR and put in my own on the same subject (A *Funny Thing Happened...*). I cued it up and asked Mitchell about the infamously fraudulent "Earth out the window" scene, with the Apollo 11 astronauts removing the fake Earth transparency from the window. I asked Mitchell what was going on in the sequence. He called the revealing segment "an aberration on the film". Mitchell then went on to anxiously say that I was wrong with my assertions, all the while he continued to smile very nervously. As an avowed atheist, Mitchell had no problem swearing on the Bible to his lie. When I pointed out to him that he was (at the time of the filming) the first Apollo astronaut to formally swear an affirmation of the matter on a Bible, as in a legally binding deposition, Mitchell became even more nervous and began to stutter.

Sitting with near the now highly befuddled astronaut was one of his sons, Adam Mitchell. It was when I made a sincere plea directly to his son that he should know the truth about his father, that Mitchell became very angry, as the Apollo astronauts' own families were likely duped with the rest of Americans as to the authenticity of the Apollo missions, no doubt for their own protection. Like Aldrin, Mitchell threatened to sue me if I shared his revealing interview with anyone, then immediately backpedaled when I gave him my card to do so, telling him that I looked forward to exposing the fraud in open court, as debating the actual facts of the matter in a legal forum, with the astronauts under oath, along with the testimony of professional filmmakers affirming the film studio electrical lighting, is the last thing any of them would want to do.

The astronaut's son then tried to assert that my interview of his father, with its challenging questions to expose this fraud, was somehow more "unethical" than the faking the Moon missions themselves. I rebutted by telling him that lying about the missions is what is genuinely unethical. After this, Mitchell said "I don't hit people", and then lied about this only five seconds later, when he did exactly that, when my back was turned to him, by angrily kicking me in the butt for exposing this monumental fraud of his. As the cinematographer and I left to pack the camera in the car, which was parked in his driveway, he and his son followed us out and threatened to go back inside and get a gun to shoot us. Some "peace guru", eh?

In all the commotion I inadvertently left the wireless microphone I was using for the interview in Mitchell's house attached to him. Additionally, my cameraman left the tape in the camera still recording when he put the camera on the back seat of the car. Without our knowing at the time, once the astronaut and his son returned inside their home, a recording of their additional private conversation had been made. It wasn't until a few weeks later, when all of the astronaut interviews were transcribed for the executive producer, that I was made aware of what the Apollo astronaut and his son had talked about privately after Mitchell had so violently, and literally, kicked me out. When our production secretary told me what the two had covertly discussed regarding me, in the privacy of their home, which the wireless microphone still attached to Mitchell had inadvertently recorded, I really thought that she was joking. She reiterated their private remarks again, and I still didn't believe her. This went on for about three or four more rounds, until I finally realized that she was serious, so I pulled out the tape to listen to it myself.

Mitchell and his son Adam were plainly heard privately discussing whether or not they would telephone their covert contacts at the CIA and have me assassinated! Really! The question is, if they really went to the Moon, and I am just some silly person who believes otherwise, rather than a serious investigative journalist uncovering a really outrageous government fraud, which I consider to be highly illegal and treasonous, then why would the CIA need to kill me in order to stop the investigation of... nothing? Sadly for Adam Mitchell, He died in 2010, at the young age of twenty six. The Bible even says that an underserved curse will fall back on the person who issued it.

The executive producer of my films came up with the idea of making a short film spoofing the secretly-recorded CIA assassination threat, as odd as this may seem. Being the kind of "zany" and creative person that I am, I liked the idea, so we produced such a movie and added it to the end of *Astronauts Gone Wild*. Some thought that this was too unconventional and believed that it detracted from the seriousness of the lethal threat, while others thought that the short comedic film about the CIA assassination threat was well placed at the end of this film about the conniving Apollo astronauts. There are actually *two* versions of this film, the shorter one, which appears at the end of *Astronauts Gone Wild*, and the longer "Director's Cut", which is my personal favorite and is available at **Sibrel.com** and click on *Moon Man* link #8.

Not too long after I had completed *Astronauts Gone Wild* in 2004, on the thirty-fifth anniversary of the first Apollo fraud, as the "punch" video made the rounds on various news programs, one of the national news networks had a special appearance of the crewmembers of Apollo 11, standing in front of the White House. As I watched the live segment from my home that morning while eating breakfast, I was surprised that, for the very first time, Buzz Aldrin did the least amount of talking of the three, as if he were losing his soulless condition, which Neil Armstrong had just recently gained. When the news anchor, who was talking to them via satellite, said that he was glad that he was interviewing Aldrin from a distance so that he would not get punched, Aldrin just looked down at the ground, ashamed.

One of my military intelligence officer friends had warned me just a few days earlier that my first film, A *Funny Thing Happened...* did not "rock the boat" in the Pentagon nearly as much as

Astronauts Gone Wild did, which made the federal government's
"secret society" members look so bad. As I sat there and watched
the crew of Apollo 11's brief thirty-fifth anniversary remarks live
on national television, a belated wave of fear suddenly came over
me. I said to myself, "They're standing in front of the greatest seat
of corrupt government power in the entire world... and it's me
they're talking about... the man who's rocking their boat. Oh my,
what have I done?!"

You would think that I would have had the sense to experience this well-placed fear long before now, yet my eternal opti-
mism, knowing that I was in the right, and strong confidence in
my 'special friends' and Creator's protection, kept my mind off of
this jeopardy almost entirely, except for my short-lived Atlanta adventures when I first found the condemning footage. I concluded
this brief conversation with myself as I watched the news segment
that morning by saying, "What I am doing is *dangerous.*"

Shortly after this occasion, when I shared with my secretive
good guy government friends my recently inspired concerns, they
reassured me that they had everything under control, so I trusting-
ly continued my clandestine association with them. I asked them
why the CIA, who obviously monitored my telephone calls about
this matter, never secretly warned any of the Apollo astronauts of
my real motives prior to my revealing interviews with them.

These special military intelligence friends informed me that,
since my covert operations with them had commenced after my
late night debriefing in the hospital, our retaliatory operations
had great effect and caused the opposition to back off. Additionally, they shared that most federal government agencies, including
the CIA, are filled with a majority of patriotic citizens who feel
that they are serving the good of their country, and that this new
generation of mostly honorable CIA employees, the few of whom
know about the Apollo deception, find it incredibly disgusting.
Because of this, they let the astronauts fend for themselves. Furthermore, if any obvious recourse were instigated against me at
this point because of my films, it would only bring undue suspicion of the fraud to the public, as well as newer employees of

this spy agency, whom tenured superiors want to keep in the dark about this matter.

As mentioned earlier, today, hopefully older and wiser, I may not have even made *Astronauts Gone Wild*, as it even makes me a little squeamish to watch it. Additionally, not only was it Biblically inappropriate for me to rebuke an older man harshly as in the case of Aldrin (1st *Timothy* 5:1), a the same Christian friend who pointed this out (albeit after the production of the film) also mentioned that, from a Biblical perspective, worldly oaths are sinful because of their "secret society" origin, and that instead a person should simply be asked to speak the truth. ("Let your 'Yes' be yes, and your 'No' be no. Anything added to this is from the Devil." *Matthew* 5:37) As such, it was not appropriate for me to have asked these men to take an oath in the first place, inciting them to lie to even a greater degree than they had before. Nevertheless, as many observers have pointed out, my follow-up film does serve as a historical testimony of the Apollo astronauts' duplicity and their dying devotion to their lifelong deception against their fellow citizens.

Only ten of the twenty-four Apollo astronauts remain alive as of this writing. Four who falsely claim they walked on the Moon and six who falsely claim they left Earth orbit to circle the Moon, which of course cannot even be accomplished today. The youngest is eighty-four and the oldest is ninety-three. Prayerfully, one of them will come forward, before it is too late, to help save not only himself, but the nation and all of humanity as well.[15]

**"The painful Truth from a friend,
is better than flattery from an enemy."**

– Proverbs 27:6

Chapter Nine
Eyes Closed – Mouth Opened

It has been prophetically proclaimed in the scriptures that, "Most people *have eyes that do not see, and ears that do not hear.*" This is likened to a household saltshaker always being placed in the same spot for fifty years; left kitchen cabinet, on the left side of the third shelf. If a family member inadvertently moves the salt shaker to the same left kitchen cabinet, likewise on the third shelf, yet on the *right* side instead of on the left side, other family members do not see it, even though it is right there in front of their eyes. It is *hidden in plain sight,* yet *not seen* due to years of programming. Likewise, I was looking at the same pictures of the alleged Moon landings over and over again for a full decade as an ardent supporter of the missions, every single day on my bedroom wall, yet still not noticing the obvious inconsistencies and abnormalities that would quickly give away the deception, *if only I would look beyond my many years of repeated* conditioning.

Real Sunlight – Note the parallel shadows – Author's photo.

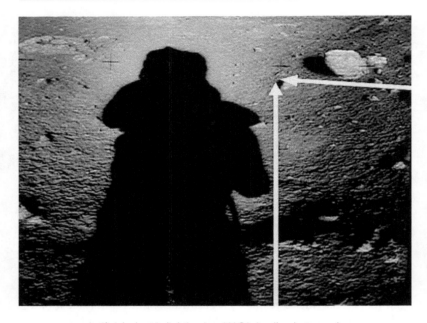

Artificial, electric lighting in a NASA Apollo photograph
Note the intersecting shadows.

The above picture, allegedly taken on the Moon in *sunlight*, was obviously **not** taken on the Moon *at all*, rather in a photographic film studio illuminated with electrical light. In fact, all that you need to prove the entire Moon landing fraud is this *one* photograph, with its ninety-degree **diverging** shadows, which simply cannot be duplicated in sunlight, which always casts **parallel** shadows. All that you have to do is go outside at high noon on a cloudless day, have yourself and a friend stand about five feet apart from one another, in the same positions as the above rock and "astronaut" are, and you will see quite plainly that the two *sunlit* shadows will never, ever intersect, and certainly not at *ninety degrees* when they are only five feet apart from one another.

Parallel shadows *always* occur in sunlight because the light source (the Sun) is so incredibly distant and large (one *million* times greater in volume than the Earth) that it casts shadows in the same direction over an entire continent (or Moon), so that no matter where you stand (or place a shadow-casting object) the shadows will *always* run parallel. However, if an *electrical* light source is used, because it is so close and so small compared to the Sun, then if one person (or object) is to the left of the electrical light, and the other is to the right of it, this difference in position, relative to a small electrical light source, may cause diverging or intersecting shadows, *just as they did in some of the Apollo images*, which proves, beyond a doubt, that the NASA pictures were taken with *electrical* light, thusly inside of a photographic film studio on Earth.

Take it from a filmmaker whose nearly forty-year career has been centered on making *fake* scenes *appear real*. This is precisely why I recognized that NASA's alleged lunar surface pictures were in fact taken in a photographic studio, and why arrogant university professors do not, who know nothing about the art of photography or filmmaking. As such, because of the *intersecting shadows* in some of these NASA photographs, which should have run *parallel* if they were really taken in *sunlight* on the Moon, I am absolutely certain that the supposed Apollo lunar surface pictures were illuminated with electrical light, and thusly taken inside a film studio here on Earth.

Additionally, as the sunlight on the Moon is estimated to be *twenty times* brighter than it is on Earth at high noon, because it has no dense filtering atmosphere, then the last thing that an astronaut would need, if they were *really* on the Moon, would be any electrical lighting for their photography, plus the fact that NASA itself acknowledged that it did not provide any electrical lights for this very reason, nor did they have the necessary battery power to run such lights.

In the iconic photo below, it is possible to see that the lunar soil near the astronaut's feet and in the foreground is darker, suggesting the surface is falling away slightly towards the photographer's position, and while the lunar soil in the background is unquestionably a darker shade of blue, it's also visibly darker in tone than the central area where the figure is standing. This is not possible on a relatively level surface, evenly lit by full sunlight. (Later versions of this image posted online have corrected this contrast difference in order to diminish the likelihood of the falsehood being discovered.)

Aldrin Standing on a studio lunar landscape (AS11-40-5903) NASA.

The most significant whistle-blow within this image is the fact that (as has been demonstrated conclusively in previous research by others) the position of the camera above the surface of the Moon *was at the same level as the alignment of the horizon line extrapolated across the visor* of the astronaut. The photograph was taken from a position higher than it should be in this situation. It was taken from eye level, and not by the astronaut, as has also been demonstrated in previous research.

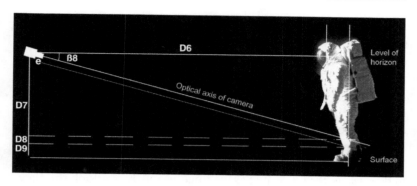

Reproduction of analysis by David Groves PhD of the camera height in the Aldrin photo indicating that the image was taken from eye level and not from the chest bracket.
(reproduced with permission)

Notwithstanding the impossibility of using the Hassleblad camera at eye level when wearing a space helmet with two convex tinted visors, we know this because *the reflection in 'Astronaut Aldrin's' visor shows that 'Astronaut Armstrong' has the camera mounted on his chest bracket, too low to record the image.* Furthermore, as the official record states that there was only one Hassleblad camera on the lunar surface with these two astronauts, it can only be concluded that the supposed photographer of the image is neither of these two astronauts.

In addition to the lighting and other "errors" within the Apollo imagery (some of it obvious like the darker areas of the lunar surface in the background), is perhaps best understandable for the following reasons.

Firstly, there is this fundamental fact that bears repeating ad infinitum until it sinks in: NASA (as well as all of the world's other space agencies) can today only fly their astronauts a distance of a mere two hundred and sixty miles above the Earth, or only *one-thousandth* the distance to the Moon, even with five decades of better technology than in 1969. Secondly, there are my personal experiences which add to the list: the recorded audio of the CIA secretly prompting the astronauts to reply to NASA after their falsely created long-distance-radio-delay in that unedited, "Not for General Distribution" film reel that I discovered. Thirdly, there is the recorded audio of an astronaut secretly discussing my assassination by the CIA, specifically because I am exposing this deception, which would not at all be necessary if astronauts had really walked on the Moon. In a way, like naïve Adam and Eve, you can't blame people for initially being deceived, after all, which is a more pleasant realm to live in, one in which your country continually lies about history and spending, or one in which your country is honorable and honest? Naturally, most people would prefer to live in the latter, *so they believe the latter*, just as we unconsciously overlook the flaws in a new romantic acquaintance with whom we are emotionally infatuated.

My infatuation with the Apollo myth ended at the open-minded age of fourteen, after seeing the revealing interview with former NASA contractor Bill Kaysing. Ten years later, when I had become a filmmaker and fortuitously happened to be editing a film one day for the producer of that very program which featured Bill talking about the Apollo fraud, I had asked the producer of this program, "Do you remember that man you interviewed who said that the Moon landings were fake? I'd like to talk with him."

My strange journey from being the biggest fan of the supposed lunar landings to becoming their most outspoken critic came about because I was *open-minded* and *willing to be wrong* when the evidence presented itself to the contrary of my first opinion, even if that evidence was unpredicted, unprecedented, alarming, and very disheartening.

Hitler, a master of propaganda, said that it was actually easier to get away with a *gigantic* deception rather than a small one, because small lies are commonplace, and therefore anticipated, yet no one would expect or foresee the audacity of a grand deception. This is precisely the psychological tactic that was used by the CIA in precipitating and maintaining the monumental, yet very simple, lie of the Apollo missions.

During the domestically injurious riots protesting the Vietnam War, president Nixon decided that a unifying pep rally of a perceived successful Moon landing was just what the sickly American patient needed. Do you really think that Nixon was going to risk killing three "National Heroes" on live television shown worldwide, when simply failing to rescue a few kidnapped hostages would permanently ruin a presidency (and especially a potential second term) as it did for President Carter a few years later? How then could Nixon *guarantee* a successful Moon mission, especially when it was technologically impossible at the time? Simply to stage it – just like a skilled poker player's bluff. In fact, Bill Kaysing (who worked for six years on the Apollo program with the highest of security clearances) had personally read and edited a classified interdepartmental memo from the rocket designer Wernher von Braun, who estimated that the likelihood of a successful manned lunar mission, on the first attempt, with 1960s technology, was a mere *one in ten thousand chance.* According to Kaysing, NASA's own staff readily admitted that their standard motto in such instances was, "*If you can't make it, fake it.*" Kaysing said that many employees regularly joked that NASA stood for "**N**ever **A** **S**traight **A**nswer." Ralph René liked this nickname so much that he regularly used it in his book.

Some wrongfully *assume* that if the Soviet Union (Russia) or Chinese intelligence agencies found out that the American Moon missions were fraudulent they would immediately "spill the beans" (tell the truth) to the rest of the world, without giving this highly significant information any deeper thought than that. This is simply not the case, and again, thinking only one step farther than programmed to do, reveals the *actual* truth. If wars are created for the profiteering of the *Military Industrial Complex*, as many forward thinking people including General turned President Eisenhower now realize, then foreign "adversaries" of the United States may only be profitable fictitious enemies thereof, and just like the Moon landings, solely exist in the minds of Americans, entirely created by the CIA's deceptive mainstream media outlets. Projects undertaken to benefit the military contractors, who in turn, help get their like-minded politicians elected, thus perpetuate this endless cycle of lucrative lies which mutually feed corrupted bureaucrats and corporations alike, about which Eisenhower so sternly warned his fellow citizens in his final televised address.

Think about this. America has been engaged in a profit-able war of some kind for *ninety percent* of its short history, yet never with Russia or China. As such, Russia and China are, in fact, *allies* of the United States, despite the CIA's mainstream media fabrications which portray them, for financial gain, as "adversaries", as trillions of dollars in annual mutually beneficial trading with these two countries proves. (This is just like a fake wrestling match in which the supposed animosity between parties is completely choreographed, when both sides are actually friends who are profitably paid by the same corporation.) This being the case, China and Russia would not bring the truth of such an American scandal as the Apollo fraud into the light (as both these nations likely *do* know the truth, yet have not exposed it) in order not to injure such an important monetary trading partner, as that would affect their own finances, plus the fact that their own hidden skeletons would then be forced out of the closet in retaliation. Any "bad blood" the United States *appears* to have with these foreign powers is simply staged, just like the Moon landings were, in order to keep trillions of dollars in profitable military spending flowing.

Alternatively, supposing that China and Russia were indeed true enemies of the United States, they still would not expose the truth about the Apollo missions, simply because this embar-rassing information could be used for greater profit than simply acknowledging it, by blackmailing the US government, adminis-tration after administration, with the highly scandalous informa-tion. For example, if I had a picture of a famous world leader with a prostitute, would it be more profitable for me to give the picture to the media for free, or would it be more profitable for me to blackmail the entrapped world leader, year after year, with ever increasing demands? If Russia and China were true enemies of America, and had proof of the Moon landing fraud, it would cer-tainly serve their interests *much more* to keep such knowledge to themselves and to blackmail the US government with the compro-mising information, year after year, in order to get the behind-the-scenes negotiations to favor them, whether it be in trade, arms, debt, or anything else. This is yet another good reason why the truth coming out about this government fraud would be beneficial for America. It would put an end to blackmail about this long ago matter by any foreign powers.

The fact is, there were no "independent" tracking stations for the Apollo missions. Any foreign entities that had such capability were affiliated to the United States' own government agencies who orchestrated the deception to begin with. One example of fooling such ground stations was the Soviet Zond 5 unmanned mission of 1968. It was initially thought to be manned, because the Soviets retransmitted the voices of their cosmonauts (who were on Earth) from the Zond 5 satellite as it went around the Moon. Therefore, to fool anyone with the technology to track Apollo, all that NASA needed was to send an unmanned probe to the Moon (which they have already done) in order to mimic the supposed location of the Apollo spacecraft, by relaying their telecommunications from an unmanned probe in this same manner. In fact, the retired NASA flight director Gene Kranz recently acknowledged, **"Our computers could tell no difference whatsoever between a 'real' and a 'simulated' Moon mission."**

From the CIA's information-controlling Wikipedia regarding the Apollo Fraud: Some people insist that the Apollo moon landings were a Cold War deception of the Nixon administration. However, 'empirical evidence is readily available to show that manned moon landings did occur. Anyone on earth with an appropriate laser and telescope system can apparently bounce laser beams off three retro-reflector arrays reported to be left on the moon by Apollo 11, 14, and 15, suggesting deployment of the lunar laser ranging equipment at asserted Apollo moon landing sites, implying equipment constructed on earth was transported to the surface of the moon. In addition, in August 2009, NASA's lunar reconnaissance orbiter claimed to send back high-resolution photos of the estimated Apollo landing sites. These government issued pictures show not only what is reported to be the faint shadows of the descent stages of the lunar landers allegedly left behind, but also apparent tracks of the astronauts' walking paths nearby in the lunar dust.[16]

At first glance, these appear to be relevant arguments, yet each one is, surprisingly, most easily and unconditionally refuted with only a modicum of further investigation beyond the initial, life-long conditioned interpretation. It is also important to know that thanks to employees "whistling-blowing", it has recently come to light that United States spy agencies regularly use *Wikipedia*, as well as *hundreds* of other websites, for deceitful misinformation purposes. In an attempt to conceal their own wrongdoing, these corrupt factions of government agencies can anonymously post intelligent *sounding* pro-government thesis to the masses, intentionally contradicting and smugly belittling truthful evidence which exposes their *very real* crimes against their fellow citizens.

The fact that billions of American's hard-earned tax dollars are being spent each and every year by corrupt elements of the United States government's federal agencies for the very purpose of concealing their own past wrongdoings, by investing in so many covert media resources that perpetually lie to their own citizens through the internet and news media, is utterly disgusting and beyond criminal. In fact, at the time of writing, if you enter "Moon Landing Hoax Proof" into a Google or *YouTube* search, you get the *exact opposite* of your request, rather a long list of links and videos that *reassure* the beguiled public of the fake Moon mission's authenticity instead!

When people use statements like "*empirical evidence* is readily available to show that the manned Moon landings did occur," it not only shows their arrogance (which, in and of itself, demonstrates their blindness to perceive reality) it also exemplifies their desperation to make an argument that is losing so much ground, that they have to resort to the juvenile tactic of claiming that if you don't agree with them, you are somehow deficient in intelligence. Again, if the landings were so obviously real, and if there is no robust proof *whatsoever* of the missions' deliberate falsification, then it follows that there would be no need *whatsoever* for the hundred plus films and websites solely dedicated to *reassure* the public of the Moon landing's genuineness! These propagandized films and websites took tens of thousands of hours to produce, and the very fact that they exist, is *proof itself* that mounting evidence *does exist* which *demonstrates* that the Apollo missions were indeed a NASA/CIA fabrication, otherwise the deceptively claimed "obviousness" of their authenticity would speak for itself, without the repeated need of hundreds of websites and videos to perpetually defend them. When a structure needs such continual precarious support and maintenance, this *alone* shows that the structure itself is *not sound to begin with.*

In regard to the *alleged* reflectors left on the lunar surface by Apollo crews, as mentioned by *Wikipedia* as a defense, firstly, it is a fact that on May 9, 1962, seven years before the first Apollo lunar landing was supposed to have occurred, a laser was bounced off of the Moon and received back on Earth by American scientists at MIT *without a manmade reflector thereon,* simply due to the natural reflectivity of the lunar surface.[17]

While it is my opinion that NASA cleverly designated naturally reflective locations as Apollo landing sites for the very purpose of contriving this so-called evidence, it is also the case that placing retro-reflectors onto the lunar surface does not necessarily require an astronaut. Russia demonstrated this un-manned robotic capability – twice, when they landed their Lunokhod roving vehicles equipped with retro-reflectors in 1970 and 1973. These were specifically *un-manned* rovers because they would not suffer the biological ravages of lethal space radiation en route nor on the surface, which is one of the main reasons NASA was, and still is, unable to send humans beyond low-Earth orbit. See Sibrel.com *Moon Man* links #9 and #9B. In the article I have referenced, you can read for yourself how deadly and impenetrable space radiation is beyond the safety of low-Earth orbit, where the International Space Station currently resides at an altitude of merely two hundred and fifty miles above the Earth, with the Moon being two hundred and thirty-nine thousand miles away on average.

Additionally, seeing how all of these lasers have their data controlled by computers, it would only take one CIA computer hacker to manipulate the information shown on a viewing screen, making even the employees of NASA ignorant of the actual facts. This was precisely what was done at Mission Control during the faked lunar landings, where dozens of computer operators actually just sat there and read the pre-fabricated *simulation* data on their screens, openly admitting afterwards that they could tell no difference whatsoever between a "real" flight and their numerous "*simulations*". You can witness this for yourself at the beginning of A *Funny Thing Happened...* right before the rocket explosions segment, where you can clearly see all of NASA's ground crews, just seconds before supposedly going to the Moon for the very first time, merely kicked back in their chairs simply watching a television presentation, just like the rest of the world was doing at the time.

Secondly, to argue that additional "new" photographs from NASA are evidence that prove the authenticity of the Moon landings is absolutely laughable. NASA and the CIA already faked high resolution, full body pictures of astronauts supposedly standing "on the lunar surface" fifty years ago, so now, with five decades more advanced Photoshop technology, faking additional pictures of such simple things as supposed tiny shadows of lunar landers, or faint footprints, or alleged trails which look like scratches on the photographs, all of which were supposedly taken from the same corrupt government's "Lunar Reconnaissance Orbiter satellite", would be so, so easy to fake. The first batch of these "Apollo site images" were released on July 9, 2009, during the elliptical commissioning orbit which was 18 miles off the lunar surface at its nearest approach – although NASA states that these "new" images were taken at 15 miles off the surface. I am sure nowadays they would be capable of seeing much, much more detail than this, *if* the Apollo equipment was *really* there, as even "private" *two hundred times cheaper* Earth orbiting satellites such as GeoEye-1 are capable of reading the print of a rooftop sign from space at an altitude that is *seven hundred times higher* than these deliberately fuzzy supposed lunar orbiting satellite pictures. Diehard Moon landing believers are just seeing what they want to see, like a naïve spouse of a cheating partner, accepting the fox's evidence that they did not steal a chicken.

Additional arguments against the Moon landing fraud are reported to be the hundreds of thousands of people throughout the industry contributing in various small ways to the Apollo project, all of whom *allegedly* would have known of the fraud and kept it a secret. Again, *seemingly* a reasonable argument, yet, with only a *little* extra thought, it is *not argument at all.* Do you really think the agencies involved would be so careless as to tell hundreds of thousands of low-level employees the goings-on of a Top-Secret project? The CIA would not really be so inept as to tell the person making a command module hatch, or the glove or the boot of the spacesuit, that they were *really* secretly faking the Moon landings and to be sure not to tell anyone! Furthermore, to say that *"because my uncle worked at NASA and believed the 'Moon landings' were real, is proof that they were real"* does not fly either. This is like saying that because my uncle worked as a vendor at the Super Bowl and believed that the game was honest, that this is *proof* that the football players did not cheat to win their game.

Just like a pyramid of power in any business, what the employee, the manager, and the regional manager knows about the business' *actual* activities and agenda, is *completely different* than what the CEO at the very top knows. Remember, there were only *three* people who were *actually supposed to be on and around the Moon at the time* of each Apollo mission, **with no independent press coverage whatsoever.** As demonstrated in *A Funny Thing Happened...* the three Apollo 11 crewmembers were in the module on top of the rocket, in my opinion, they did launch into Earth orbit (in order to go up in front of witnesses, splashdown in front of witnesses, and to attain realistic "zero gravity" flight photography from within the spacecraft), yet for the rest of the mission, everything beyond Earth orbit was completely contrived, like a masterful illusionist, with satellite data manipulation, complete media control, and professional movie sets.

After all, what is easier to do, to *actually* build a rocket in 1969 and travel to another heavenly body on the very first attempt, or simply to construct movie sets in a highly-secure film studio with a detailed script, director, a crew and a special effects department?

The age-old argument "*the simplest explanation is the true one*", which many naive Apollo proponents deceptively use to suggest that the Apollo missions were real, *actually proves the fraud instead!* The simple fact is, it is considerably easier to *fake* such a mission than to *actually accomplish one.*

Another overlooked fact is that according to the scientific method, in order for any new accomplishment to be considered *authentic*, a scientific *claim*, such as the alleged 1969 manned lunar landing, *must* be peer reviewed. That means *independently verified and duplicated by at least one expert third party*, in order to be verified or deemed *genuine*, which has **never** *happened with the supposed Moon missions.* Only NASA has claimed that this feat was even possible, even though fifty years later no nation on Earth has ever repeated the supposed achievement, including the government which claimed they did it on the first occasion. This is precisely why, if someone today made the claim that they had successfully achieved cold fusion, yet said that they could not repeat their *alleged* success for at least another *fifty years*, they would be laughed at and dismissed as fraudulent, yet this is **not** the same reasonable scientific *standard* that is applied to the claims of the US federal government concerning the alleged Moon landings. As I have already said, this is simply because the supposed lunar missions have become a *god* to its believers, who are one hundred percent closed-minded to any other interpretation, and thusly incapable of considering **any** genuine and condemning evidence of the fraud.

Some of the best evidence proving the fraudulent lunar landings is the fact that in 1997, as already stated, when the Space Shuttle Discovery spent eleven days flying from between three hundred and sixty miles, to three hundred and eighty five miles altitude (roughly *fifty percent* higher than the Space Shuttle normally flew) mission control needed the crew to descend to a lower altitude as soon as possible due to the level of deadly space radiation that they encountered near to the beginning of the Van Allen radiation belts, that were still more than two hundred miles away. That is to say, this 1997 Space Shuttle crew was only two hundred and thirty-five miles *below* the inner belt and when flying over the

South Atlantic were within the inner belt. The crew reported that they could see sparks of light hitting the retinas of their closed eyes, which was attributed to the highly radioactive, and higher than normal, space environment.

Discussing this surprise radiation, a naive CNN reporter inadvertently, and unknowingly, acknowledged the Moon landing fraud by stating, **"The radiation belts surrounding Earth are more dangerous than previously believed."** What is *"previously believed"* if not *based on the previous false reports of the "harmless" radiation belts from the Apollo crews,* who were allegedly the *only ones in all of world history* to have ever traveled through them, without suffering any ill health effects whatsoever. Apparently, not a single journalist on the entire planet figured out, *except for myself,* that this statement *totally contradicts* the authenticity of the Moon landings.

The only time human beings have *claimed* to have traveled through the deadly Van Allen radiation belts is during the *alleged* Apollo missions. All other manned space missions, from every country, including the US, have all orbited *below* this dangerous radiation zone *specifically out of safety concerns for this lethal radiation above them.* Even airline crews, flying some two hundred and forty miles below the Space Station are subject to health concerns from this hazardous radiation.

The inner belt is not static and solar wind activity can even affect lower altitudes than that of the International Space Station. This is why airline crews wear radiation detectors that are checked regularly, so as to minimize their exposure, as airline crews are susceptible to receiving even more deadly radiation than someone who works in a nuclear power plant. Even at the altitude of the Space Station, which is *three hundred and seventy miles below the lower edge of the inner belt*, the crews there receive the equivalent of a normal four-year dose of radiation in only *ten days*.

How is it then that shuttle astronauts in 1997, spending most of their eleven-day mission at the median altitude of three hundred and seventy-four miles, discovered more about this lethal radiation than the Apollo astronauts did *30 years earlier, who supposedly went much higher than this nine previous times?* According to the highly-esteemed National Research Council, a private nonprofit scientific think tank which submits recommendations to NASA based on the latest scientific findings, radiation beyond Earth orbit is so dangerous that *"returning* to the Moon" is deemed **impossible** until the necessary technology is *developed* to protect astronauts from this lethal radiation. The question is, if the National Research Council says that *"returning"* to the Moon is *impossible today, until the technology is invented to protect astronauts from lethal space radiation beyond low-Earth orbit,* then how did NASA's primitive virgin 1960s technology reach the Moon without adversely affecting the crews as a result of the deadly radiation exposure, seeing how the National Research Council just acknowledged that the equipment necessary to do so has *yet to be invented?* Or better still, rather than reinventing the wheel in order to protect today's astronauts from this lethal space radiation, why not simply use the same outstanding methodology and equipment that the supposed first Moon crews did?

It really is quite a conundrum that thirty years before the Space Shuttle, with untried 1960s technology, NASA claims to have gone **so much farther** than the more advanced Space Shuttle ever did – *all* without any fatalities or radiation-induced health problems whatsoever. **Do you still believe that the Moon landings were real?** Please check out Sibrel.com *Moon Man* link #8C.

When Bush Jr. was president in 2003, he went on national television and proclaimed, "*The United States will return to the Moon as a logical first step to Mars and beyond.*" Did no one besides a few ardent researchers like me notice that if they already had *really* been to the Moon *six* times, then why in the world would they need to do a "*first*" step over again for the *seventh* time? Bush Jr. went on to say that "We will put a man on the moon by 2020." Am I, again, the *only* journalist in the entire world to wonder why, with 1960s technology that predated VCRs and cell phones, that it only took *eight* years to go from scratch to walking on the Moon, yet with five decades of far more advanced technology, it takes *seventeen years* of *new* development to repeat a *fifty year older* technological claim?

Wake up people!

After seven long years of technological development towards Bush Jr.'s Moon goal (only one year less than the claimed 1960s timeline), an independent scientific government panel determined that NASA was so far behind schedule to reach the Moon, even with decades of better technology, that the panel estimated that it would be *sixty-six* years after the alleged first moonwalk (2035) before NASA had the capability to repeat the original claim!

Additionally, every five years since the alleged lunar landings, many presidential administrations have said that they would "return" to the Moon, yet none of them has ever accomplished this, even with *eight* different proposed timelines! At the time of the writing, NASA says that the agency will, for the *ninth* yet-to-be-fulfilled time, "return to the Moon by 2024". Have they not reviewed their own scientist's independent 2009 findings which conclusively state that it is impossible for NASA to "return" to the Moon before **2035**? Trust me, and their own independent scientific panel, NASA will either postpone, for the *ninth* time, any returning to the Moon, or sadly have to fake it yet again.

In 2016 NASA said that it would have the, far more advanced than Apollo, unmanned Orion spacecraft "orbiting the Moon by 2018", yet NASA could not even do this, and no one seemed to even notice their *tenth* unmet Moon goal. Amazing isn't it, that with virgin 1960s technology NASA claimed that it had astronauts walking on the Moon only eight years after President Kennedy's goal, yet their own scientists say that it will take **fifteen years** instead of eight to figure out how to "repeat" the task, even after having *allegedly* done it before! For some strange reason, their first goal to reach the Moon with untried technology was **ahead of schedule,** and now repeatedly with considerably more advanced technology, NASA has **never** kept **any** of its **eight** deadlines to "return" to the Moon!

Do you still believe that the United States government had men walking on the Moon in 1969 on the very first attempt?

In 2010 President Obama was even so bold as to pose the question, "How do we shield astronauts from radiation on longer missions?" Am I the only journalist curious enough to ask and repeat ad infinitum, "Why not do it the same way that worked so well the first time they went to the Moon way back in 1969?" Why does no other journalist connect the *obvious* dots with this very revealing information? *Because the dots lead to a horrific truth that would appall the entire American nation, who would then demand that their entire government be reconstituted or replaced.* It is simply because mainstream journalists are part of the CIA's media empire that they do not report anything like this that would cause their own downfall.

In December of 2014, NASA sent its new Orion spacecraft, *un-manned,* directly into the Van Allen radiation belts and then promptly returned it to Earth for study. According to NASA, the purpose of the Orion mission was "*to test the instruments.*" What "*instruments*" were onboard the Orion spacecraft? *Two Geiger counters to measure the radiation inside of the belts, which have to be passed through to reach the Moon.* Didn't NASA already have these measurements *fifty years ago* from the Apollo missions, if indeed astronauts *actually* went through the radiation belts to the Moon and back? Why is it so important to "*test the instruments*" *inside* of the radiation belts? To see if humans can survive traversing it *for the very first time!*

Apparently today's new generation of NASA engineers, some in their twenties, have stumbled upon these significant NASA contradictions. Though they were probably led into the space exploration field by the motivation of the seemingly easy, successful Moon mission of 1969, the fact that such an acclaimed feat has not been repeated to date, and that aside from the alleged missions of the Nixon administration, no astronaut from any nation has ever left low-Earth orbit, these startling realizations must make their NASA jobs quite precarious.

Kelly Smith, one of these twenty-ish engineers, was selected as the official Orion radiation mission spokesperson in the NASA video press release showcased below. Notice that at two minutes forty-five seconds into the film (2:45) Smith confirms that the radiation belts are made up of **"Dangerous Radiation"**. At time 3:35 Smith plainly states, **"We MUST solve these (radiation) challenges BEFORE we send people through this region of space."**

The question is, and I have to ask it again, if the solution to the dangerous radiation belts problem has *not yet been solved* ("We *must* solve these challenges *before* we send people through this region of space") then how is it that the Apollo crews, during their alleged Moon missions, successfully went through this *"dangerous"* radiation, when a NASA employee just admitted that the necessary equipment to survive doing so has **yet to be invented?** Please see **Sibrel.com** *Moon Man* link #10. **Did Kelly Smith reveal this obvious contradiction accidentally or intentionally?**

When I asked NASA's press office if I could interview Kelly Smith about this radiation matter, they refused to grant me permission to talk with him. When I emailed NASA a list of mostly harmless questions about the Orion mission, the agency quickly answered all of them. When I submitted a more difficult inquiry concerning Kelly Smith's three statements about the "dangerous" radiation of the Van Allen belts and how the radiation problem *"must* be solved *before* NASA can send astronauts through this region of space", NASA refused to reply to these questions, *as if I had never asked them.* When I asked NASA for the *radiation readings* of the Orion spacecraft's two onboard Geiger counters, they said that such measurements were *"a government secret".* When I asked them why such ordinary information about nature is a secret, NASA refused to answer this question and then terminated all further communication with me.

When NASA sent citizen-funded probes and spacecraft to measure the temperature of the Sun and the amount of hydrogen in Jupiter's atmosphere, this information was readily available to scientists and the public alike, after all, why would a measurement of a part of nature be a "government secret?" Likewise, as the amount radiation in the Van Allen radiation belts which surround the Earth is simply a part of nature, there should be no reason whatsoever why such elementary measurements of nature are a "government secret"... *unless ... disclosing such measurements would reveal the impossibility of the Apollo missions.*

James Van Allen, the discoverer of the radiation belts, originally said that they were,"*One hundred times more radioactive than a lethal dose*" and "*One thousand times* more lethal than expected.*" [emphasis added] Under pressure from NASA, he dramatically recanted his original findings in order to make it *appear* as if the Apollo missions were technically possible. The link below shows Van Allen's original published findings in the respected national journal *Scientific American*, in which he plainly spoke about the radiation belts beyond Earth orbit being "an obstacle for practical space travel to the moon and beyond", just as Kelly Smith of the Orion mission reiterated. Van Allen himself said this in 1958, immediately after NASA sent probes with Geiger counters into the radiation belts:

> Our measurements show that the maximum radiation level as of 1958 is equivalent to between ten and one hundred roentgens per hour, depending on the still undetermined proportion of protons to electrons. Since a human being exposed for two days to even ten roentgens would have only an even chance of survival, the radiation belts obviously present an obstacle to space flight.[18]

The above comments are at the very end of the article linked here. To read this important article see **Sibrel.com** *Moon Man* link **#9B**.

Occupational safety limits for radiation here on Earth is 5 REM *over an entire year*, and the danger level is estimated relative both to the amount of REM *and* the period over which it is received, and thereby gradually absorbed, so that the body may have time to incrementally expel the radiation before it reaches a lethal level. The Apollo spacecraft only had so-called radiation shielding that consisted of paper-thin *aluminum*, while a medical x-ray technician wears a much more effective *lead* vest (lead being prohibitive to launch into space due to its excessive weight) even though by comparison, the radiation exposure to an x-ray is only *one-five-thousandth* of the radiation exposure from the Van Allen radiation belts, and an x-ray is only for a fraction of a second, while the radiation belts exposure would be *continually for some two hours* during the journey to the Moon and another two hours on the return journey. Some misinformed NASA Moon landing fans who were grasping at straws, have falsely claimed that the supposed Apollo trajectory to the Moon did not take it through the radiation belts at all, while others claim that the purported Apollo trajectory only took it through the outer parts of the radiation belts. The fact is, NASA itself has claimed for decades that the Apollo astronauts went right through the middle of the radiation belts (as shown in the agency's own press releases of the alleged trajectory), as there is no way to zigzag around them, because launching the rocket closest to the equator as possible (southern Florida) – where the radiation belts are strongest – uses the least amount of fuel to achieve orbit.

What these diehard fans of the Moon landings have inadvertently done is admit that *yes indeed the radiation belts are deadly*, just as Van Allen and NASA's own Kelly Smith acknowledged in the Orion radiation mission video press release. When these misled NASA disciples desperately claim that the Apollo crews went "around" the deadly radiation belts, in a forlorn attempt to prove that the Apollo missions were real, they are actually acknowledging the lethality of the radiation belts, while at the same time unknowingly conceding that the missions to the Moon were scientifically impossible, since NASA's own Kelly Smith now openly admits that the technology necessary to successfully travel through the deadly radiation belts *has yet to be invented*.

Remember self-proclaimed Moon astronaut Alan Bean? How he was so unprepared for my challenging questions that he accidentally admitted *on camera* that he did **not** travel through the radiation belts, and when I pointed out this error in his story, Bean corrected himself by saying, "*Maybe* we did [go through the radiation belts]."

In another twenty-first century NASA video, a Space Station astronaut also admits that low-Earth orbit still remains the technological limitation of NASA's manned spacecraft (because of the radiation issue). He even accidentally says that NASA *hopes* to "*eventually*" send astronauts to the Moon. To see this admission see **Sibrel.com** *Moon Man* link **#11**.

Another item that is trotted out as alleged proof that the faked Moon missions actually happened, is the existence of all those lunar rocks that they supposedly brought back from their travels. In August of 2009 it was reported, albeit as a news oddity (and it certainly was) that an alleged "moon rock", personally given to the prime minister of the Netherlands by Neil Armstrong in 1969 (who supposedly hand picked it off of the lunar surface himself), was opened forty years later from its (presumed permanently) hermetically sealed container by a curious museum curator after he had watched *A Funny Thing Happened...* with great interest. Following his microscopic examination, the rock was verified to actually be a forgery! It turned out to be a deceptive "out-of-this-world looking" piece of *petrified wood*. Yet again, not a *single* journalist, *except for myself*, asked the question, "If the moon rocks are fake... what does that say about the Apollo missions?" This is precisely why owning a "moon rock" is a felony, so that none of them can be examined independently. In fact, a seventy-five year old woman was even arrested by federal agents for being in possession of an extremely tiny supposed "moon rock" the size of a gnat, which was trapped inside of a thick clear paperweight (so that it could not be easily opened and examined), that had been given to her deceased Apollo engineer husband by Neil Armstrong as a souvenir. To read the story about the fake "moon rock" see Sibrel.**com** *Moon Man* link #10B. And to read the story about the "moon rock arrest" see

Moon Man link #10C.

After Neil Armstrong's apparent departure from this life in 2012, his widow found a bag of "Moon souvenirs" in the back of his closet. The problem is, for Armstrong's *entire life* he said that these *specific items* were *left on the Moon!* Again, *more proof* that the alleged Apollo missions took place *on Earth* was *deliberately ignored* by the CIA's mainstream media. Visit **Sibrel.com** *Moon Man* link #**10D.**

Even more proof of the Moon landing fraud is the fact that, according to NASA itself, all of the blueprints of the hypothetically miraculous technologically-advanced hardware that allegedly put a man on the Moon on the very first attempt in 1969, was *deliberately destroyed* after the supposed missions, as was all of the technical specifications of the spacecraft, along with all of the flight data that recorded the spacecraft's *actual* location during the missions. You would think that such, one-of-a-kind, supremely valuable and expensive designs with all of its irreplaceable data, would be kept for just short of all of eternity, both as a record of the achievement and in case such costly-to-attain information and equipment would be needed again to return to the Moon. Yet the **exact opposite** is true. See **Sibrel.com** *Moon Man* link #**12.**

How did the very basic onboard computer, calculate *in real-time*, communicating exchanges with Earthbound computers, manage the precise rendezvous with the LM, which started at zero miles per hour as it supposedly launched from the lunar surface, and then allegedly synchronized itself perfectly with the height and speed of orbiting command module, which was supposed to be traveling at three thousand miles per hour around the Moon, all without missing each other even by a fraction of a second, which would have had fatal consequences for the crew in the returning Moon lander? **No one will ever know.**

How did the LM power its air-conditioning nonstop against an outside temperature of 252° Fahrenheit (122° C) down to an amazing 72° Fahrenheit (22° C) inside of a spacecraft sitting on the lunar surface for three days with what were, essentially, a bunch of car batteries? **No one will ever know.**

Imagine Bill Gates spending two hundred billion dollars to

build the first computer, and then once successfully completing it, throwing the computer and its blueprints into a furnace.

Would anyone ever - ever - ever do such a crazy thing? Of course not.

Yet this *is* what NASA did with its "amazing Moon technology" on the very first try. **This is proof *itself* that the Apollo missions were fraudulent.** Has anyone *ever* deliberately thrown away breakthrough technology in the entire history of the world? **Never.** Even the atomic bomb, though this technology perhaps *should* have been discarded after its first use, was *cherished with relish,* protected with all security, then *multiplied and improved upon one hundredfold within just ten years.*

Another simple example of this fact is the impressive B-52 bomber aircraft, which was first invented over *seventy* years ago, and worked so well that it is *still* in use today by the United States Air Force. If the alleged Apollo equipment **really** worked as claimed, then NASA would **never, ever** throw away all of that money and time invested into producing it, which would only force it to reinvent everything from scratch all over again in order to "return" to the Moon. Additionally, if NASA *really* sent men to the Moon so easily, then there would certainly be bases there *right now* due to the Moon's strategic and scientific importance. The fact that there are *not* bases there right now is simply because *it cannot be done,* not now, and certainly not with 1960s technology. It is that simple.

On the other hand, if NASA *faked* going to the Moon, and a detailed analysis of the engineering specifications would reveal that the rocket was not capable of leaving low-Earth orbit, and even less able to land and survive on the Moon, then yes indeed, NASA would *definitely* destroy any and all proof of its Moon landing deception, **which is *exactly* what this government agency did.** Therefore, the very fact that NASA *did* destroy the evidence of its claimed Moon missions is ***proof itself*** that the agency did *not* actually achieve them. Just as wise King Solomon knew by the person's behavior who the actual mother of the child in question was, as one woman defended the baby's life and the other did not, we can tell by the US government's *behavior* in destroying the *evidence* of the Moon missions, that they were *indeed* falsified.

Also notable is this statement made by Wernher von Braun and his two colleagues concerning the original mathematical calculations these highly intelligent rocket designers considered as being the *only* way for astronauts to reach the Moon. This necessary methodology was not adopted by NASA, nor even closely adopted, simply because it was far too difficult to achieve, as it is to this day. I read this out loud to Eugene Cernan as you can see in *Astronauts Gone Wild*:

> It is commonly *believed* that men will fly directly from the Earth to the Moon, but to do this we would require a vehicle of such gigantic proportions that it would prove an economic impossibility. *Calculations have been carefully worked out* on the type of vehicle we would need for the nonstop flight from the Earth to the moon and to return. The figures speak for themselves: Three rockets would be necessary, each rocket ship would be taller than the Empire State Building and weigh about ten times the tonnage of the *Queen Mary*.[19] [emphasis added]
>
> – Wernher Von Braun, Willy Ley, Dr. Fred Whipple

In comparison to the above requirements, the rocket that the United States government *claimed* sent astronauts to the Moon in 1969 was the Saturn V. It weighed just two thousand five hundred tons versus the stipulated eight hundred thousand tons of the *Queen Mary*, which is a difference of **thirty-two thousand percent.** Instead of reaching the required height of one thousand two hundred fifty feet as per the Empire State Building, it was only **three hundred sixty-three feet** tall... and there was just **one** rocket, instead of the necessary **three.** Furthermore, von Braun went on to say that **before** a manned mission to the Moon, an Earth orbiting space station must **first** be constructed from which to ferry the three rockets and the necessary additional fuel for the long voyage all the way to the Moon and back. Von Braun further *insisted* that immediately after landing on the Moon, crews would have to find or dig a cave in which to shelter themselves from *thousands* of micrometeorites *per hour* hitting the lunar surface, which travel at speeds *in excess of twenty thousand miles per hour*, that would inevitably puncture the spacecraft, as well as the astronaut's spacesuit, causing catastrophic, and *fatal*, environmental decompression. This of course, like the numerous other requirements, was *never* done.

When the CIA told Wernher von Braun to *"adjust his numbers a little bit"* in order to reflect a fictitious way to reach the Moon with the available technology of the 1960s, he obediently and immediately, recanted his previously published calculations by a factor of **thirty-two thousand percent**. Did I mention that this man in charge of the Moon landing program, Wernher von Braun, was brought to America specifically by the CIA and was a former World War Two *Nazi SS Officer*, of whom the USA's own government's State Department is on the record for saying that had he not prematurely died shortly after the Apollo project, he would have been immediately thereafter indicted for war crimes, for overseeing the genocide, *and the cover-up thereof*, of hundreds of innocent people during WWII? This threat of blackmail, and probably bribery as well, was undoubtedly used to gain von Braun's obedient submission to the federal government's Moon landing deception, as well as his subsequent "adjustment" of *irrefutable* mathematical calculations. ("The figures speak for themselves.")

The specifications, blueprints, and flight data of the miraculous 1960s Moon landing technology (which NASA *intentionally destroyed)* were not the only important materials relating to Apollo that "mysteriously disappeared". The original videotapes can be added to this list as well. In 2005, after three years of initial research between Australia and the US, it was discovered that all the raw Slow Scan TV footage (the video originals) of the supposed moonwalks had been recorded onto 1-inch magnetic tape by the Australian observatories and were boxed up and sent to the Goddard Space Flight Center (GSFC or Goddard) as stipulated by NASA. During the search it was ascertained that Goddard had not recorded the arrival of these tapes according to the prescribed protocols. After Apollo, Goddard had sent all the boxed Apollo data to the federally-secured National Archives. However, by 1984, at the specific request of Goddard, all but two of these boxes had been returned to them. While their departure from the National Archives was recorded, a notation of this return does not exist at Goddard. Subsequently, all of this one-of-a-kind irreplaceable material is now considered *"mysteriously lost"*. This includes the original Apollo 11 SSTV recordings of Man's historic first steps onto the Moon. By 2005, even employees at the Johnson Space Centre (JSC) could not find the original Apollo 11 footage. By 2006, it was concluded that only Goddard holds the answers to the question, "Where are the original Apollo videotapes?" *Why* they are missing is obvious to anyone reading this book.

During the time spent searching for these NASA originals, the 2005 documentary *Magnificent Desolation: Walking on the Moon in 3D* was produced. According to my sources, the inability to find these original moonwalk videotapes could have something to do with the fact that the filmmakers had asked NASA for the *original* Apollo videotapes of *all* of the supposed lunar surface coverage. The reason for the request was so they could be transferred onto high definition film in order to be able to be shown, for the first time ever, on an IMAX® screen, which was nearly one hundred twenty feet wide, *for all the world to see at a resolution that was at least six times greater in detail than had ever before been witnessed.* If NASA's own employees cannot get a hold of any Apollo originals, then it was a certainty that the producers of this film were not going to be successful either, even if it was a pro NASA film. In fact, there was so little actual *original* footage available of the claimed "greatest event of mankind", that it is said that the director had to resort to renting VHS tapes of the alleged Moon missions from Blockbuster Video, in order to have at least *some* version of the vanished NASA footage! The director of *Magnificent Desolation* was so disappointed with the low quality of the VHS images which he was forced to use, that in order to minimize the now *umpteenth* generation VHS diminished quality, he reduced their video size within the nearly one hundred twenty foot wide screen to only about *five percent* of the available space. Consequently, when the documentary commemorating the supposed missions was finally produced – without this essential material – the production had resorted to filling about *ninety-five percent* of his landmark film with *reenactments* or *recreations* of the alleged moonwalks, which were likewise created in a film studio.

In case you were wondering "what if", someday, the mysteriously vanished original videotapes of the Moon missions were to one day miraculously be found?... Oops!... Did I forget to tell you? The *only* machine on the *entire planet* that could *ever* play these one-of-a-kind format videotapes *was* to be found – at Goddard! In Goddard's Data Evaluation Lab that was closed in October 2006.

Halfhearted proclamations have been made about trying to preserve this rare equipment, just in case those original Apollo videotapes are ever found, yet based on Goddard's past unscrupulous behavior in this matter, this seems highly unlikely. In fact Eugene Krantz, flight director for the first mission, has openly stated, "We could not even play the tapes if we found them because those machines have been disassembled." But then hurray! In 2019, NASA asserted that nothing had been lost after all – as such. Well, yes, they couldn't find the *original* videotapes, as these must have been *erased and recorded over*. Which is pretty amazing, considering the value of their content, had it been a *real* event. NASA stated that:

> There was no video that came down slow scan that was not converted live, fed live, to Houston and fed live to the world. The data on those tapes, including video data, were relayed to the Manned Spacecraft Center (now the Johnson Space Center), during the mission.[20]

All this is true, yet it is not the core issue. No one is looking for second hand scans of the SSTV footage. They are looking for the original very high quality slow scans that were supposedly coming from the Moon, and in particular for the SSTV footage

from Apollo 11. NASA's statements on the matter are in direct
contradiction to the data in the report, and rather begs the questions as to why MSC (or JSC as it is now known) were trying to
access the original SSTV scans back in 2005, if they already had
everything they needed since 1969?

Funny, isn't it? NASA continues to spin the agency's corruption in such a way as to make the intentional destruction of such
historic irreplaceable materials seem reasonable to the public. Unless one knows how these images were generated and collected
from the get-go, one might even believe NASA's contrived version
of these hard-to-believe events, such as the falsified Moon landings themselves. The only conclusion that can be drawn is that
due to the inauthenticity of the Apollo missions, no one, not even
NASA employees planning future lunar missions, are ever going
to see the original SSTV video images in their purest form, just in
case improved video technology has the ability to reveal the fact
that the Apollo missions were *actually* filmed on Earth inside of
a film studio.[21]

When various other nations and private enterprises finally,
after *fifty years* of trying, have the technological capability to send
microwave oven-sized *unmanned* probes to the Moon (*still no human crew due to limitations of the technology and the inability to shield
from the lethal space radiation*) the United States federal government quickly drafted laws to keep the *alleged* landing sites of the
Nixon administration completely *off limits to any and all third
parties.* The US government now says that even private flyovers
of these locations, and certainly any ground incursions thereof,
by any independent probes, of *any* nation, *including its own,* are
strictly forbidden. Since when does the United States federal government have to right to tell its own or the other scientists of the
world where they can and cannot explore? This can only be to
avoid any discoveries that prove that the Apollo equipment is nonexistent on the Moon. You would think that the US government
would gladly welcome independent confirmation that its incredible technological claims were *real*, especially in the face of growing
universal doubt as to their authenticity, yet again, the *exact opposite*

proves to be the case. It is like a murderer who boasts about their innocence, all the while refusing to give a personal DNA sample, which they know will convict them.

China, a trillion dollar trading partner of the United States, and also a technological leader, has sent *un*-manned probes to the Moon. As all of the Moon is uniformly desolate and one landing site is just about as good as any other for exploration, as it is almost entirely unexplored, I would think that the *perfect* and most logical place to land would be that of the United States' alleged first landing site, *if it really existed*, in order to prove that its probe was *really* on the Moon. The fact is, the Chinese government already knows of the Moon landing fraud (as my research concludes that this specific US deception is even taught in Chinese universities) yet as previously mentioned, exposing this fact internationally would be damaging to their trillion-dollar trading partnership with the United States, so the secret is mutually kept private. Subsequently, China steered clear of any *supposed* NASA landing sites for any of its unmanned lunar probes, even though these were obviously the most logical places to land.

Astrobotic Technology, a private firm, *had* planned to land an unmanned probe precisely at the claimed Apollo 11 landing site, as the company also saw this as the most logical place to prove that their probe was really on the Moon (as they wrongly *assumed* that the 1960s landings were real), yet because of intense pressure from the US federal government not to do so, the president of the company, John Thornton, caved in to the government coercion and reluctantly agreed not to land in that obvious location as originally planned, even though he was supposedly "free to do so." Is it scientific "freedom" when important exploration is abandoned because of government pressure to maintain a falsehood of the criminally rogue CIA? Even Israel's supposedly independent space agency submitted to this very same pressure. After its first and only lunar probe mysteriously crashed onto the surface in 2019, despite decades of improved technology, and right before taking revealing high resolution orbital pictures of the Moon's surface, the Israeli space agency strangely said, "Returning to the Moon is not chal-

lenging enough", even though they never once successfully landed there! This was their face-saving excuse for having bowed to
American pressure not to attempt to take any future photographs
of the nonexistent American landing sites.

* * *

Now I have something major to disclose. This disclosure is now possible as the high-ranking military source of my investigation into this
matter has died, and the predetermined waiting period after his death
has expired. I am now free to publish his testimony that comprises the
following highly relevant information about the Moon landing deception, which is shared here for the very first time.

My source did not want the following facts to be published
until a set time after his death because his life and the lives of
his family members were threatened, face to face, if he ever told
anyone that he had personally witnessed the counterfeit filming
of the supposed 1969 Moon landings here on Earth. In fact, just
days before writing these very words, immediately after I had re-
confirmed all of this information with a surviving family member
of this important source of mine, their home was broken into
with professional spy-like precision, their sophisticated security
camera alarm system was cleverly disabled with their own secret
password, and all of the relevant documents about this matter,
and nothing else, were stolen from their home. Two days after this
break in event, this surviving family member of my eyewitness to
the Apollo fraud was visited by two unidentified "US government
officials". They threatened his life, and the lives of his family, if
he ever spoke to me again. In order to protect this individual,
I notified the FBI, a United States Senator on the Intelligence
Committee, and the White House Press Secretary.

This original direct eyewitness of the Apollo deception, now
deceased, was the *Chief of Security* at the United States military
base where the staged Apollo 11 Moon landing was secretly
filmed. He was a first-hand eyewitness to the incredible events
that I relate below.

The year was 1968. Preparations for the first fake Moon mission photography and filming that was to take place in the United States was underway, a full year in advance of broadcasting the falsified mission to the world, in order to have enough time to fully prepare and implement the contrived material. Lyndon Johnson, the US president at the time, was personally presiding over the first of three days of filming of this sad misadventure. I was informed that this was set up inside two very large aircraft hangers that were coupled together to best simulate the fake landscape's enormity. The later missions likely used a similarly large professional film studio somewhere.

This Air Force Military Police Chief described many days, even weeks, of preparation before the filming was to take place. Countless tons of pulverized concrete were delivered to the military base in dump trucks, which were to be used as the "lunar soil" for the creation of the photographs and pre-filmed television images, while laboratory quality "test" samples of supposed lunar soil were made from crushed lunar meteorites, which had been personally retrieved from Antarctica by rocket designer Wernher von Braun the previous year.

Cannon Air Force Base near Clovis, New Mexico was the location of this filming. It was obscure, remote, quite small, and thusly would have the fewest possible eyewitnesses. Additionally, Cannon Air Force Base was also the secretive "Special Operations Command Center" for the entire United States Air Force, which is their interdepartmental equivalent of the CIA. The operation's code name was **Project SLAM DUNK.** This code name resulted from President Johnson's private remarks about the supreme urgency of attaining Kennedy's misspoken December 31, 1969 deadline to have a man walking on the Moon, which Johnson said **"WILL be met, come hell or high water"**, in order to save international embarrassment. "Come hell or high water" obviously included the faking of the missions, in order to *ensure* that this goal was met. As the prefabrication of the planned Moon landings **absolutely guaranteed** that the technologically impossible lofty goal was met on time, the once impossible Moon missions were suddenly transformed into an easy "Slam Dunk".

Below are fifteen names of visitors that the Chief of Security at Cannon Air Force Base was personally given by President Johnson, who were permitted to enter the highly-secured secret government military facility to observe the filming of the fake lunar landing. The names are listed below in the exact same order as they originally appeared on the list that I received from the Chief of Security at Cannon Air Force Base. President Johnson's name was at the top of the list, followed by astronauts Neil Armstrong and Edwin "Buzz" Aldrin. This could mean that they were only there to observe the event, in order to attain a general familiarity with what was going on, so that they could later recall it as if it was a personal experience. The two "astronauts" could have had doubles standing in their place or they may have done it themselves or perhaps both. The list does not include certain military personnel and all the photographic and film industry professionals such as the full crew, set designers, model makers and special effects people etc. They used a separate entrance and were on a separate list, which is not available at this time.

Lyndon Johnson – President
Neil Armstrong – NASA Astronaut
Edwin Aldrin – NASA Astronaut
Wernher von Braun – Rocket Designer
Robert Emenegger – Image Consultant
Eugene Kranz – NASA Flight Director
James Webb – NASA Administrator
Joseph Kerwin – Future NASA Astronaut (flew in 1973)
Thomas Paine – NASA Deputy Administrator (in 1968)
Glynn Lunney – NASA Flight Director
Christopher Kraft – NASA Mission Control Founder
James Van Allen – Radiation Expert
Arthur Trudeau – Army Intelligence
Donald Simon – Unknown (Navy)?
Grant Noory – Unknown (CIA)?

I was informed that these specially equipped top-secret film studios, along with all the mountain backdrops, the studio sets, as well as all the film and photographic equipment, were quickly disassembled after the photography and filming was complete so that no trace of it remained. Even the fact that President Johnson once visited Cannon Air Force Base, which at one time was boasted about on the Air Force base's website, was quickly removed after this investigation into the matter commenced.

When the Chief of Security of Cannon Air Force Base saw the supposed "live Moon landing" on television a year later, he said that he cried quietly in sadness, yet still justified the deplorable deception to himself, as the rest of his fellow participants did, as a "necessary military bluff" in order to appear to be superior to Russia's more advanced space technology at the time. The fake Apollo missions were also used as a much needed "pep rally" for disheartened Americans, who were perpetually disgruntled over losing tens of thousands of their husbands, brothers, and sons in a needless foreign war in Vietnam, which itself was entirely instigated by another CIA deception, the completely contrived "Gulf of Tonkin attack on American soldiers by North Vietnam", which was entirely fabricated as the *excuse* for entering the war in the first place.

The CIA's own historians and other Pentagon officials finally admitted to the "Gulf of Tonkin *deception*" in 2005. If it weren't for the monumental international embarrassment and sharp decline in the United States dollar and stock market that would likely follow the public disclosure of the Moon landing fraud, then this deception would have otherwise been admitted by now. Just keep in mind, if the CIA and the United States federal government were willing to **kill a million people** in a war that would have otherwise not been entered into without their **deliberate deception** to justify it, then I am sure that they are willing to simply fake a television image.

There is so much evidence that the Moon landings were fraudulent, in fact, there is more logic and evidence to support that the missions were falsified than there is to defend them. Diehard NASA fans may try to convince you of the opposite, when all they really have to support their fifty-year old unrepeatable claim are some Moon rocks that have been proven to be false, lasers that can bounce off of the Moon without using any manmade equipment thereon, and contrived photographs whose shadows signify that they were taken in a film studio on Earth.

**"Have nothing to do with deeds of darkness,
instead, expose them."**

– *Ephesians 5:11*

Chapter Ten
Attacking the Messenger

I am sometimes criticized by my fellow citizens as being unpatriotic for saying that the alleged American Moon landings were a NASA and CIA deception, **even though this *is* actually the case.** The United States has hopelessly descended into a realm where liars are heroes, and truth speakers are villains. If George Washington arose from his grave today, and saw all of this unspeakable corruptive government deception, no doubt he would take the first ship back to England. Washington repeatedly spoke in painstaking detail of the desperateness of the situation his Continental Army were in, who were facing the vastly outnumbered and better equipped British troops. Even at that early historic hour, the *unflattering truth* was not welcomed by a congress who wanted to hear flowery *lies* of success instead of unpleasant realities of failure. Nowadays, the leaders of America and the world have gone from "I can *never* tell a lie," to lying virtually **all of the time**. It is not *un*-patriotic to expose corruption – it is **patriotic**. It is *un*-patriotic to have committed this deceitfulness in the first place. If you favor truth and love America, then you can see why the *truth* will set you free, because it is the very exposure of the Moon landing fraud that will free Americans from their bondage to the extremely corrupt United States government agencies.

I am constantly assailed by the *age-old* juvenile technique of ad hominem, attacking the *bringer* of bad news, *rather than the very real message itself*, by those who feel that they have no other course of action, because the reality of the truth speaks so loudly for itself and cannot otherwise be refuted without such diversions. The fact that my critics so repeatedly and desperately resort to attacking a *messenger* of the Moon landing deception, is proof itself that the message is truthful, otherwise they would have no need to resort to such tactics in the defense of their position, if indeed their position was not so dramatically faltering to begin with and in such dire need of misdirection from the emerging condemning evidence.

This, sadly, reminds me of the 2016 leaks of the Democratic Party leadership obtained from hacked computers and servers. Instead of the FBI pursuing the criminals who brazenly rigged a presidential primary (one in which the candidate with the most votes, Bernie Sanders, nevertheless repeatedly received the least amount of delegates), the FBI chose instead to start a prosecutorial investigation into those who merely released the condemning truthful information of the illegal act (the messengers), and did not pursue those who actually committed the unlawfulness in the first place! What a sad, sad joke of the country's systemic insidious governmental corruption, and yet some people still think that fabricating the Apollo missions, well out of sight of any eyewitnesses or independent media, is beyond corruptibility.

My term of *two years* as senior news editor and a reporter for an NBC affiliate has been falsely presented by my leading critic as *"two months"*, in an unscrupulous effort to discredit my professional journalistic experience. I should know, I worked there through two consecutive Christmas holidays and then some, so I and a dozen eyewitnesses know better than he how long I worked in the news department there. If my leading critic has to *lie* to make his argument supporting the alleged authenticity of the Moon landings, then his argument is not valid to begin with, as valid points do not need *lies* to support them. If he was simply mistaken, then his inept powers of research prove that if he cannot uncover the truth about *one* simple fact on Earth in his own country, then how could he *possibly* discern the numerous intricacies of CIA intrigue as to what may or may not be taking place *on the Moon* when he was only four years old? The great thing is, either way, his own false statements regarding such a simple matter, prove that he is wrong.

Completely fabricated, and highly outrageous, accusations have been made against me, simply for telling an unpleasant truth.

I even regularly receive vulgar curse-filled death threats. In fact, I once received an email in which the sender said that they wished that they could watch as I, together with my wife and children, were burned alive before their eyes... just for saying that I think the United States government lied to the public on at least *one* occasion! This is further proof, yet again, that the alleged Moon landings have become a god to some people, the fanaticism of which is *itself* evidence of their own hypnotic deception. The fact that people react like rabid dogs from a mere statement, is further proof that the statement is true, as a sword with no point causes no pain.

> **"The further a society drifts from the truth,
> the more it will hate those who speak it."**
> *– George Orwell*

I have received literally thousands of emails from viewers of my films about the falsified Moon missions over the years. Until about three years ago, ninety-five percent of the emails that I received were very critical of me and my work. They generally considered it "blasphemous" of me to say that the Moon landings were fraudulent. Then, for some reason, almost overnight, about three years ago, ninety-five percent of the emails suddenly became positive. This change indicates that a *Paradigm Shift* has occurred. This means that people have suddenly begun to realize that something they previously believed was true is really false, and started believing the *exact opposite* of what they did before, such as when everyone suddenly realized, or they were finally properly taught, that the Sun did not rotate around the Earth, rather that the Earth rotated around the Sun.

Here are a few positive emails that I have received.

> Bart,
> I loved your article on did NASA really go to the moon fifty years ago.
> I've also watched your films and they are awesome.
> You are very brave. It takes a lot of courage to expose these devils.
> I'm just asking you to be careful. They have killed many people for

doing a lot less than you. I'm afraid of what might happen to you if you continue to push it. I wish there were millions more just like you. I'm hoping that this younger generation will rise up, demand answers, and force a restructuring of the government, giving us leaders we can trust.

I wish I could make a difference like you have. I think you are great and I admire you. I'm praying for your safety, and I wish you all the best in the future.

Kindest regards,
Mike

Here is another,

Dear Mr. Sibrel,
My name is Stephen. I am a truth seeker and I, of course, came across your efforts in my now fifteen plus years of research. I wanted to extend to you many thanks for your efforts. It is because of you, Andrew Johnson, Marcus Allen, Richard D Hall, and Dr Judy Wood, that I continue to dig for truth. However it was YOU who inspired me. It is YOU who continues to inspire me.

As you well know, truth seeking can be very depressing, disheartening, and troublesome. Being ostracized by those who you thought loved you can make you feel completely alone in this fake world of cloak, smoke, and mirrors.

I thought about what would possibly make me feel better about my efforts if I were you, so I decided to write to you and tell you that you have inspired me and changed my life for the better.

I am fifty years old, and as a child my "hero" was Neil Armstrong. Now that I know better, in the realization that my loyalties were misplaced, I have found heroes in my above list. Thank you so much for your tireless efforts, for taking that punch, for taking that kick, and for showing us all how practicing one's rights is still at the discretion of the free individual.

Your friend and fan,
Stephen

And another,

Hey Bart,
I just wanted to say thank you and keep up the honest work. I know it's hard sometimes when everyone is threatening you for revealing

the truth. I just wanted to say that you are opening up a lot of people's eyes and that is fantastic.

Everything we've been told is a lie and it's awesome that you are revealing this truth to everyone. The videos are done so well, with astronauts actually wanting to punch you in the face to escape. How comical is that and people still don't believe.

Keep up the good work my friend.

Your brother in Christ,

Benjamin

Fortunately, the shift towards this important realization has begun. Prior to this, I was fired from a television network, excommunicated from a church, lost thousands of dollars in filmmaking work, and all of my family disowned me, all for simply pursuing what really happened regarding the Apollo missions and revealing it to a mostly disinterested, ridiculing lost world.

In 2018, about a year before any public knowledge of internet censorship, forty percent of my income as a filmmaker was discretely taken away by Google, by their banning all advertising on all of my films on their platform *YouTube*. If they publicly took down my movies about the Moon landing, it would only prove me right, so instead they secretly penalized me for revealing this deception of theirs. What their action really proves is that Google is **not** a profit-based private business as it outwardly *appears*, otherwise the company would not have *intentionally* forfeited seventy billion dollars in market capitalization by disabling ads on thousands of truth-telling films like mine, which likewise expose flagrant government and corporate corruption. The only entity that would penalize someone for revealing that the CIA orchestrated the faking of the Apollo missions is simply the CIA itself, thereby proving that Google is operated by the same. A year after Google discretely took my advertising revenue away for telling the *truth* about the Moon landings (while financially rewarding others for *lying* about them) their CEO appeared before the United States Congress and said, specifically using the Moon landing controversy as their prime example, that they were deplatforming and demonetizing such free speech as mine to instead promote

"**authoritative** content", that is, whatever those in **authority** *say*
the truth is, which is our *corrupt lying government leaders!* George
Orwell must have been a prophet.

The reason why Google's parent company is called Alphabet
Inc. is because this has long been a Pentagon byword for the federal government's conglomeration of tyrannical agencies; CIA,
NSA, NRO, FBI, IRS, DEA, DOD, DHS, etc. As I said before,
with the government's admitted "misplaced" 2.3 trillion dollars, I
believe they *purchased* Google, *YouTube*, Facebook, AT&T, as well
as many other communication and television companies, in order
to better spy on, and control, the world and their own citizens.
Central *Intelligence* means Central **Information**. Google/*YouTube*
is obviously *not* in business to make money, otherwise they would
not throw away seventy billion dollars just to rebuke those who
expose government fraud, instead they are *clearly* in operation to
control information, which is *exactly* the role of these corrupt government agencies. People at Nissan, my former primary *YouTube*
sponsor, informed me that they could care less whether or not the
people who buy their cars believe that the Moon landings were
real or fraudulent, only that they buy their cars, otherwise that
would be like Nissan saying that they only wanted to sell cars
to one political party yet not the other. For Google to **lie** and
say that the reason for cutting off my ad revenue was because my
films are not "advertiser friendly" only digs the hole deeper for
themselves, as Nissan clearly indicated to me that my films **are**
advertiser friendly, as they gladly sponsored them for several years
previously. Additionally, monstrous Google, without my consent,
just put ads *back* on all of my films, only now they keep all of the
ad revenue rather than sharing it with me, which proves *twice* that
taking my ad revenue away to begin with was *not* because my films
were not "advertiser friendly", rather was done so *punitively*.

Why this deliberate prejudicial financial penalizing for content critical of the CIA or the powers-that-be is not deemed illegal is beyond me. After all, the electric company cannot legally
turn off my electricity if I made a film critical of them, so why is
Google/*YouTube*, Facebook, and Twitter allowed to do so? They

are obviously utilities as well, just like a cable television provider, which according to federal law, are not allowed to discriminate based on race, color, or *creed*. What is *"creed"*? It is a *belief*. I simply *believe* that the Moon landings were falsified. The CEO of *YouTube* claims that the company does not *believe* this. So what? According to federal law I cannot be discriminated against, censored, or financially penalized because of my *beliefs*. Period.

Where is my Congress Member, Senator, and President when I need them? What are they all doing about my *forty percent* of lost income through **illegal discrimination**, as well as defending thousands of others who are being unfairly treated in this same manner as me? If they are doing nothing about it, then this inaction simply *proves* that these "Representatives" *are* the corrupt powers-that-be that I am exposing. "You can judge a tree by its fruit." (*Matthew 7:15-20*) Want to know which Representatives *really* represent you? Simply look up how they voted on GMO labeling, which ninety percent of Americans wanted, yet Congress and the President passed the exact opposite legislation, a law which actually **forbids** mandatory GMO labeling. If your so-called "Representatives" were **against** telling you the truth about what you and your family are swallowing, then they do **not** represent you. **They are liars.** If they voted **for** telling the truth if a genetically modified organism is in your food, then they *may* represent you.[22]

Just as Ralph Nader received coordinated attacks for exposing the corruption at General Motors, I too have received the same as the messenger of this insidious government corruption, so exemplified by the Moon landing fraud. In fact, *National Geographic* (a propaganda arm of the US federal government), in a television "Special Report", in a vain attempt to discredit my findings in *A Funny Thing Happened...* went to a Californian desert *at night* to supposedly "simulate" the alleged photographic conditions on the Moon, which were claimed to have been taken in *sunlight*. They dressed up an actor in an astronaut costume, had him stand a few feet away from another crewmember, brought in one electrical lighting source to *supposedly* simulate the Sun, and basically said, "See! The shadows of the two people standing near one another *do* intersect in our 'Moon simulation', *just like in the* NASA *pictures*, so filmmaker Bart Sibrel is wrong in saying that intersecting shadows prove the fraud."

This deliberately deceptive program falsely claimed that they did their simulation this way because, "We can't duplicate the Sun," yet they easily *could have* if they had only filmed in the very same spot twelve hours later, *in sunlight!* Only *then* they would have accurately depicted the very same *sunlit* conditions on the Moon, in which the alleged Apollo photographs supposedly took place, where the shadows would **never** intersect! If they had truthfully depicted the sunlit conditions on the Moon, by doing their reenactment in sunlight, then the clear evidence would have conclusively proved me right. This is precisely why they did their simulation in the exact opposite manner, to deceptively lead the viewer into wrongfully believing the exact opposite of the truth.

To reiterate the point I made previously, all that you have to do is go outside at high noon on a cloudless day, in sunlight, have yourself and a friend stand about five feet apart from one another, and you will see for yourself that, because the Sun is a million times bigger in volume than the Earth, that the two sunlit shadows from each person, on either the Earth or the Moon, will **never, ever intersect**.

The *National Geographic* deceptively tried to convince its viewers that both I and my film *A Funny Thing Happened...* were wrong with the exact same evidence that proves me right! Again, my point is, in their intentionally deceptive and backwards demonstration, that their shadows intersected because their Moon simulation was lit with electrical light just as the fake Apollo missions were, in which the shadows also intersected! All the while they falsely claimed that this methodology proved that the Moon missions were real, when in fact they actually proved that the Moon landings were falsified, as it was *electrical light* that caused intersecting shadows in both their "simulation" and in the electrically lit fake NASA pictures! Absolutely incredible! (You can watch this program at **Sibrel.com** click on *Moon Man* link **#13**.)

Artificial electric lighting from a *National Geographic* show unintentionally demonstrating intersecting shadows.

By the way, and not so coincidentally, the corrupt United States government openly acknowledges giving continual financial support to *National Geographic*, and I believe secretly directs or owns it for propaganda purposes, purchased with their admitted "missing" **two thousand three hundred** billion dollars, after all, he who pays the piper calls the tune. This Moon landing hoax is far from the first time, or the last time, that the CIA's "bought and paid for media" was grossly complicit in horrendous crimes against their own people. In fact, CBS's main national spokesperson for the Moon landing fraud, Walter Cronkite, speaking of the *real* role of the media, is on the record for privately saying to his fellow Masonic lodge members (of which many United States presidents, CIA directors, and Apollo astronauts belong), that **"Our task is *not* to tell the truth; we are *opinion* molders."** [emphasis added]

Days after President Kennedy was murdered (by the CIA, in my opinion), the CIA's reporter, Dan Rather of CBS (propaganda) news, went on national television to defend the CIA's actions and said **the** exact opposite of **the truth** about the Kennedy assassination. In the clip below, you will see Dan Rather *actually* report the **exact opposite** of the plain facts (just as the *National Geographic* did) when he describes his viewing of the highly damaging Zapruder Film, which clearly shows, because of Kennedy's head going violently *backwards* from the fatal bullet, that the gunman was in *front* of him, **not** *behind* him, as claimed by the CIA's "news media", in order to frame innocent Oswald, who they said was *behind* Kennedy, and whom they would also have murdered only days later, so that an open debate of the actual facts of the case would never be discussed in a public courtroom. As this revealing film of the Kennedy assassination was *deliberately* never shown on television at the time, the citizens of American were told to *trust* "admirable" Dan Rather's *interpretation of it* as he described it for them. When Dan Rather relates the scene of the fatal gunshot, in which Kennedy's head so obviously goes violently backwards, proving conclusively that the bullet came from the front from a different person than Oswald, Rather instead says the exact opposite of the truth, "His head could be seen to move violently forward".

Do you find it difficult to believe that such blatant lies would be deliberately told by the (CIA-owned) "news networks" in America? Just look at the clip below to see this **intentional** *backwards* portrayal of reality, just as Rather and fellow liar Cronkite did for the CIA during the alleged Moon landings a few years later. See **Sibrel.com** *Moon Man* link **#14.**

The super plain and simple fact is, if Oswald *actually* killed Kennedy, then the United States federal government's files on the matter would have been available for public review immediately in 1963, rather than having been surreptitiously deemed "*classified indefinitely*", which *itself* proves that there is a deception about the matter that the corrupt United States government agencies are trying to conceal, otherwise the files about it would be out in the open for all to see. It is that simple and that sad.

The clip above of the **completely** propagandized "news", which told the American public the **exa**ct opposite of **the truth** about the Kennedy assassination regarding the clear condemning evidence of in the Zapruder film (just like they did with my film exposing the Moon landing fraud), proves beyond a doubt that the CIA already completely controlled the news media back in 1963 when President Kennedy was assassinated, and so successfully thereafter covered up. This was only five years before the same CIA faked the Moon landings, and this was when there were supposed to be government regulations in place to prevent such a thing from ever happening, which have long since been abolished! Today with *legal* centralized media control, and a "missing" 2.3 trillion dollar budget to buy up all "news", "social media", and telecommunication companies, the CIA's complete control of propagandized "news" must now be **ten** to **one hundred** times more powerful and insidious than it was in the 1960s, when they already so successfully killed Kennedy, blamed an innocent man for it, and then afterwards got away with faking the Moon landings. Thusly, can you even imagine the *complete* control that the CIA's "news media" has today over people's false perception of what is really going on? No doubt, as exemplified by just these two previous examples, what the public is being told about the events of the day is undoubtedly the exact opposite of the truth. This is precisely why, out of the one thousand five hundred media outlets surveyed about their stance on the CIA's publicly acknowledged intention to overthrow the democratically elected Venezuelan government, an *amazing* **one hundred percent** of these alleged "*independent news agencies*" were all for it!

The plain and simple reason why the CIA is doing all of this, is because if the press were really "free and independent", then *real* journalists like myself would have discovered and published evidence that points to the CIA as being responsible for the death of Kennedy and the false Apollo Moon missions. If reports like this were broadcast nationwide until something was done about the CIA's blatant and unabated rogue corruption, *as they should be*, then the public would rise up and put an end to their illegal criminal hold on power, while imprisoning a lot of them. Simply put, the CIA completely controls the "news" so that this will not happen. It is no coincidence that right after President Kennedy publicly stated that it was his country's journalists who are responsible for keeping a corrupt federal government in check, that he was murdered by the same corrupt entities.

A few honest United States Senators tried to get to the bottom of the CIA's involvement in the assassination of John F. Kennedy, sadly *thirteen years later*, by forming the "United States House Select Committee on Assassinations", as they were not at all satisfied by the perpetrator's "official report", which naturally blamed someone else. It was called the "Committee on Assassinations" because these Senators easily recognized that there have been *numerous* illegal assassinations carried out by the rogue CIA, and that John Kennedy's was just one of many. This investigatory committee firmly concluded that there was indeed another gunman other than Oswald! (If he was at all to blame.) The question then arises, if one branch of the United States federal government states as a **public fact** that someone *other than Oswald* killed President Kennedy, then why has not the "respectable" FBI ever put a murderer of a United States President, who is obviously *uncaptured*, at the very top of their "Ten Most Wanted List", indefinitely until they are apprehended?

The CIA's *National Geographic* further lied in its own corrupt "official report" about the CIA's falsified lunar landings when it stated, "Only a very small group of people believe that the Moon missions were fraudulent." Really? Is **eighty-two million** people of three hundred thirty million Americans a "very small group"? It is one quarter of the population. (Add to this number the approximately **four billion** others, in other non-brainwashed countries, who already recognize this deceitful fraud.) Propaganda programs like theirs, which are perpetually trying to reinforce the sincerity of the Moon landings, are continually quoting decades older polls before vast numbers of people became aware of this despicable government crime because of films like mine. The numbers I just gave are the 2020 statistics, which, to these fraudsters' alarm, are growing daily.

If the group of people who know of the fraudulent lunar landings is so "very small", as they falsely claim, and the Moon landings are so "obviously" real, then what is the esteemed *National Geographic* doing wasting a million dollars of expensive television time trying to persuade such a "small" group of people out of their "*insignificant*" discovery? Obviously, these expensive resources are being spent because of the growing **millions** of Americans who are coming to their senses, who are joining **millions** of others, in recognizing that their *government-controlled* television networks are deliberately trying to keep them in a hypnotic slumber so as to overlook past, as well as ongoing, criminal activities of theirs. This is precisely why they make counterargument programs like these, in a desperate attempt to stop the public from waking up after their years of beguiled deception.

The *National Geographic* program's alleged "expert" as to the Moon landing's supposed authenticity, a person of such astuteness that he proved me right with the very evidence with which he was trying to prove me wrong, admitted that his life's work is to convince people that the Moon landings were real. Why would this be anyone's life's work if these missions were genuine, the evidence which exposes the fraud is weak, the number of people who recognize the deception is so "very small", and those awakened to the reality of their scientific impossibility with 1960s technology are just "crazy", as the program insinuated? Would you spend your entire life's energy trying to convince insane people who thought that the country's first president was Mickey Mouse that it was really George Washington? Of course not.

The amount of time, energy, and resources that are regularly spent on this and a hundred other films, television specials, and websites, specifically created to convince supposedly defective simpletons of the alleged "obviousness" of the claimed Moon landings, speaks for itself as the deliberate propagandizing of a lie. If something so continually needs to be maintained against the unpleasant emerging realities of its deception, and if all of the evidence of the fraud were not so factually compelling, then such desperate measures would not have to be taken to defend something that is supposed to be "obviously" truthful. When a structure needs such continual precarious support and maintenance, this itself is evidence that the structure being perpetually defended is not sound to begin with.

Even the scene in *A Funny Thing Happened...* in which the astronauts appear to be "floating" around in one-sixth gravity, is so obviously a simple, yet very effective, "slow motion" effect, that when the *National Geographic* showed the same clip from my film in their deliberately deceptive propagandized "Special Report", *which was specifically created to disprove my damaging film*, they deliberately zoomed in on this condemning footage (enlarged it), far beyond the soles of the astronaut's feet and the dirt on which they walked. This was intentionally done so that viewers could not see that the astronauts were only getting the same half an inch off the ground as they do here on Earth, which my film specifically exemplifies, and which they deliberately covered up.

If this were not damaging proof of the fraud, then they would have no need to *deliberately* **enlarge the original video to conceal this evidence!**

When you simply double the speed of this Apollo 11 footage with professional video equipment, as I did in *A Funny Thing Happened...* it becomes blatantly obvious that the seemingly convincing "one-sixth gravity floating effect" is nothing more than a rudimentary, yet effective, "slow motion" effect. Truly, *this alone*, proves that they were not on the Moon, where they should have been able to leap several feet off the ground. (They occasionally accomplished this in later missions, with hidden cables, newly developed in order to overcome this initial oversight on their part.) Again, the *National Geographic* program's deliberate concealment and misrepresentation of all of these facts itself proves that my assertions are true, otherwise they would have no need to cover up and distort these things!

The equally duplicitous propaganda television program *Myth Busters* used the very same *deliberately deceptive* methodology as did the *National Geographic* program, by lighting their simulated moonscape with *electrical* light *inside of a film studio* rather than using easily available *sunlight*, as the comparable conditions were supposed to be, in order to make it appear as if intersecting shadows and other lighting anomalies were "normal" in NASA's falsified pictures allegedly taken on the Moon, which were likewise taken with electrical light inside a studio. This is precisely why their misleading "experiment" with electrical light matched NASA's TV pictures. If they really wanted to present the truth, then they would have obviously done their "Moon reenactment" in sunlight, as the NASA pictures were claimed to have been taken in sunlight. Had they actually used the easily accessible *sunlight* outside their own building to simulate the *sunlit* conditions on the Moon, by merely walking ten feet out their door, then they would have conclusively **proved the fraud instead**, as I have shown, sunlight produces parallel shadows and electrical light produces intersecting shadows. The fact that they deliberately chose not to do this, is direct proof of their intentional complicity in perpetuating this cover-up. This is precisely why they used electrical light to replicate the NASA pictures. Again, these liars proved me **right** instead of wrong, all the while they tried to deceive their audience into believing the **exact *opposite* of the truth**, just as Dan Rather did. Incredible!

When I pointed out these deceptions of theirs to the producers of these two programs, who had originally asked for me to be interviewed on camera in their programs, both program's producers withdrew their invitation, or deleted my previously recorded interviews about this, because not only did I prove that the missions were fraudulent beyond any doubt, I also exposed their intentionally misleading methodologies designed to make their counterfeit claims to a beguiled public, something they were not about to allow me to do on national television.

If two television programs about the Moon landing fraud conspiracy "theory" refuse to have on their show the *world's best known investigator of this very subject*, and *deliberately deletes from their content conclusive evidence of the fraud* that was supplied to them by him, then *this itself* proves that I am right, because if the Moon landings were so "obviously real and incontestable" as they falsely claimed, then they would let me speak uncensored about their own fraudulent methodology used in their argumentation, plus show the newly-discovered (and highly condemning) unedited video evidence without any fear whatsoever, which neither of them dared to do. Thusly, the final *lie* of theirs was that these programs were an "open debate of the issue", rather than their sole purpose *really* being to reassure the doubting public that this age old deception of theirs is still trustworthy, despite overwhelming mounting evidence to the contrary. I guess this is why such a broadcast is called a "program", because they are *programming* the minds of viewers to *believe* their lies and to *obey* their commands, and they do not want anyone like myself coming along to rewrite their hypnotic mental software.

Do you see how *upside-down* reality is portrayed by the CIA's television "news", where *misrepresentations* are presented as *truth* and where *truth* is presented as a *misrepresentation?* The real "myth" is that Moon landings took place on the very first attempt, even though they cannot be repeated by anyone, even fifty years later. *This* is the *myth* that they should be busting. Instead, they are a propaganda arm of the corrupt United States government's CIA, whose native language, as spies, is *lies*, all the while they charged the citizens under their care two hundred billion dollars for the privilege of being lied to about the Moon landings. Utterly disgusting. **Do you have eyes that *truly* perceive... or only eyes that see what the magician *wants* you to see?**

NBC, my old alma mater, for a program on their affiliate the Discovery Channel, paid me thousands of dollars, flew me to New York City, put me up in the upmarket Waldorf Astoria hotel, all because a new, independent-minded producer of theirs wanted to televise my side of the story, as well as exclusively showcase the first network broadcast of my unedited video evidence of blatant behind-the-scenes photographic deception from the first alleged Moon mission. (Remember, another NBC news director, who had previously viewed the very same footage, decisively said that it conclusively proves the fraud, though disappointedly added, "I cannot broadcast this. It will cause a civil war".)

After filming my interview and transferring a copy of the footage in preparation for a special national broadcast about the Moon landing hoax, everything suddenly, and mysteriously changed. Obviously, the less honorable agents of the CIA, through their telephone and email monitoring, had found out about this unprecedented program that NBC was preparing to broadcast, and which the producer had tried to keep a secret until then.

This new NBC producer told me that NASA had somehow found out about their revealing program (which was supposed to be in confidential development) and as retaliation threatened NBC, as well as all of their other networks (like the Discovery Channel, the Si-Fi Channel, the Weather Channel, Bravo, USA, E, Oxygen, Fandango, Hulu, and Comcast) with never cooperating with them – *ever again*, on any space-related program, as well as *permanently disconnecting their live camera aboard the* International Space Station, if they broadcasted this revealing television program of theirs with my condemning footage of false photography from the first alleged Moon mission.

Sadly, NBC succumbed to NASA's blackmail, cancelled their Discovery Channel television special showcasing my amazing discovery of behind-the-scenes footage of fake NASA photography, and never broadcast the interview they had painstakingly filmed of me meticulously explaining this newly uncovered evidence. As NBC had already enthusiastically purchased the exclusive rights to my discovery, it cost them tens of thousands of dollars to cancel the program they had already produced about the fraud, specifically sidelined to appease the very perpetrators of it, which only proved to those involved in the production of this forbidden television special, that NASA was obviously guilty of staging the Moon landings, just as I had said and my footage proved.

Do you still believe there is a free press outside of government control?

The only television program to ever broadcast my unedited film footage of the in-flight fake Apollo 11 mission photography, along with its highly-revealing secret audio channel of the CIA prompting the astronauts during their deception, was Tech TV's enormously successful national cable talk show called "Unscrewed", who inadvertently broadcast the revealing footage without prior executive approval. In fact, this show was so popular, that their viewership doubled every thirty days for the first three years it was on the air! Despite being the highest rated program on their entire network by far, bringing in the owners of the channel untold millions of dollars, the show was abruptly canceled immediately after broadcasting this inflammatory footage of NASA's fake photography, after someone powerful higher up witnessed the studio audience reacting to my discovery with incredible horror and indignation when they saw the revealing footage. This cancellation was a not so subtle warning to other broadcasters, who might be tempted to make the same error of judgment. Since then, knowing this penalty of termination hanging over their heads, no other network has dared to broadcast any portion of this incriminating evidence, which emphatically proves, to both a NBC news director and a NBC news producer, as well as to many other filmmaking professionals, that the alleged Moon missions never left Earth orbit, which is still their altitude limit today, even after fifty years of more advancements in space hardware and computer technology.

I even met privately with "investigative journalist" Geraldo Rivera in New York City, in order to personally give him a copy of *A Funny Thing Happened...* with its video evidence. While I later appeared as a guest on his show to discuss this topic, Geraldo made it clear to me that though he may be personally suspicious of the Apollo mission's authenticity, he is not able to say so publicly and keep his job. The only way that I could appear and present my case on his program was if I did **not** show the number one key piece of evidence of the fraud, the fake filming of the "Earth halfway to the Moon", which proves that none of the Apollo crews ever left Earth orbit. Why would this important one-of-a-kind evidence of the fraud be forbidden from being broadcast if the astronauts *really* went to the Moon?

Instead of showcasing this absolute proof of the deception, the producers of "Geraldo" chose instead to sensationalize the violence I received in pursuit of the truth.

The same is true of *The Washington Post*, the newspaper that broke the infamous "Watergate" scandal. While this publication interviewed me in-depth on the topic of the fraud, the story which they actually wrote was about "how interesting it is that some people doubt the Moon landings", rather than an *actual investigation* into the real possibility that indeed the missions were a Cold War CIA deception, who then later used the allocated money for illegal Vietnam War purposes. When I asked the reporter assigned to me about the condemning video evidence of the astronauts openly staging their photography of being halfway to the Moon, along with the revealing peculiarity of the hidden audio track of the CIA prompting the astronauts to fictionalize a four second radio delay, in order to falsify their distance from the Earth, the *Washington Post* reporter paused for several seconds quietly and then reluctantly replied, "**I can't explain that**". This "investigative journalist" then went on to say that such an investigation along these lines, while it might prove to be radically true, would nevertheless result in the termination of his employment with the publication.

Is this in any way *freedom* of the Press?

USA Today, along with numerous other prominent national newspapers, magazines, television, and radio stations, all ran stories in which they allegedly "reviewed" my documentary – *all without actually watching it!* (They told me this themselves.) The only exception was *The Washington Post*, which after *actually* watching my film about the fraud, admitted that they were completely dumbfounded by the video evidence it contained, yet still wrote *absolutely nothing* about this incredible discovery, which two high-ranking news producers already admitted was *absolute proof* of the fraud! Whenever I tracked down the person who wrote these numerous critical reviews of my movie and asked them, "What did you think about the unedited footage of fake filming aboard Apollo 11 showcased in my movie?" they *all* replied a paraphrasing of the following (except for *one* who wrote nothing about it for fear of being fired), "Well... I didn't *actually* watch the movie. I wrote the review based on the concept of the film, not the actual content."

Ninety-nine percent of alleged professional "journalists" for major newspapers, television stations, and magazines, actually wrote reviews about a film which they did not even watch! Can you believe it? Why aren't these people fired for incompetence or dereliction of duty, instead of being promoted to positions of national media authority? These people repeatedly refer to me as "crazy" in their writings, without even contacting me for an interview or even watching my film. Writing about a film you have never seen, and a living person you never contacted for an interview, is what is truly crazy. NASA claiming that the agency sent astronauts one thousand times farther than they can even send them today, is what is truly crazy. These naive zealots that the CIA's media digs up to combat every occasion in which the truth of this corruption pushes into the light of day is a perfect example of Lenin's "useful pawns" quotation.

In the year of the notorious fiftieth anniversary of this government fraud, I was hired by forward thinking inspired independent producers to host and be the leading investigator of the six episode television special *Truth Behind the Moon Landing* for the Science channel (I suppose that title was chosen to add false credibility to their government propaganda). Even though I was unanimously selected by an independent panel as the most logical and capable choice to host the program and to be its leading investigator, and already contractually hired to so do, I was fired at the last minute by the secretive CIA owners of the network, specifically because I did *too good of a job* proving the deception! I so successfully refuted all of the faltering arguments to defend the *un*-scientific dying myth that inept 1960s "science" put a man on the Moon that the non-truth-seeking "science" channel refused to broadcast the program if I was allowed to present my irrefutable evidence of the falsified Apollo 11 mission.

In fact, their bogus investigation, *allegedly* into whether the Moon landings were real or not, opens with this statement taken from their own website: "One of America's greatest achievements is also one of its most controversial. Now a team of 'experts' investigate if there was a conspiracy to fake the Moon landing."

First of all, how can their program actually be an accurate investigation into the reality, or not, of the alleged lunar landings when they start off by saying "One of America's Greatest Achievements", thusly already concluding from the very beginning that the government claim was authentic? Secondly, how can their person who is *supposedly* on the side of "we did *not* go" *really* be an "expert" when no one in the "we did not go to the Moon" community has ever even heard of this individual, plus the fact that the most recognized and qualified person available to *truly* represent this point of view is banned from their program, even after all the producers unanimously chose him?!

Thirdly, for their so-called "expert" to imply that the Van Allen radiation belts are not lethal and therefore easily traversable, and no impediment whatsoever to human beings reaching the Moon (despite NASA's present-day scientist Kelly Smith contradicting all of these points) actually proves that he is the *exact opposite* of a knowledgeable authority on the subject. This contrived "expert" of theirs took a very small *ever so slightly* radioactive coin (which was so harmless that it could be handled), placed it on one side of some flimsy material similar to that used on the Apollo spacecraft, and then put a Geiger counter on the other side of it. Getting no significant radiation reading from the tiny harmless sample, it was falsely suggested that the 1969 shielding had performed adequately to protect the lives of the Apollo astronauts from the lethal radiation of the Van Allen radiation belts. Using only the *slightly* radioactive coin the size of a quarter is like comparing the weight of a fly to the weight of an elephant. If my interview refuting such weak argumentation had been broadcast, rather than deliberately censored, then you would have heard me make that simplest of rebuttals about this *intentionally deceptive* and juvenile "demonstration" of theirs. I would have also shown the video of NASA's own Kelly Smith stating that these radiation belts *are indeed* deadly and that the technology needed to travel through them successfully has **yet to be invented**. Of course, they never showed Smith's comments or mine about this, proving that they had no intention whatsoever of *genuinely* investigating the authenticity of the alleged Moon landings, rather that their program's purpose was to *recondition* the viewer into accepting the government's lie.

Therefore, the fact that they *deliberately terminated* the most recognized critic of the alleged authenticity of the Moon landings from hosting their program, even after all of the producers had already unanimously hired me to do so, specifically because I would have shown on national television that their contrived "experts" are really fraudsters, is *proof itself* that the Moon landings were a hoax, because if they were real, then not a *single* piece of my evidence would prove otherwise and they would have *gladly* had me on their program to show everyone what a "fool" I am.

It is laughable that they proved me right whether I hosted their program or not, because if I was allowed to speak, as all of the producers wanted me to, I would have proved the fraud. Banning me and my evidence *also* proves the fraud, because if astronauts *really* went to the Moon, then they would not have a solitary thing to fear from me appearing on their show. Deliberately removing me and my evidence from their so-called "serious investigation" of the matter, simply demonstrates that there is indeed a cover up.

If George Washington really was the first President of the United States, then no one in the world would spend an entire year making a six-part television series to defend such an obvious fact. If they *really* went to the Moon, then not **one** minute of precious and expensive airtime would be wasted to convince "idiots" otherwise, much less six one-hour broadcasts. In the past, the CIA's media would make a single one-hour program every five years to keep the Moon landing lie going and the growing truth to the contrary at bay. With the fifty year anniversary of this *still* unrepeatable 1960s claim bringing the falsified Moon landings to the forefront of people's minds, and because today there is mounting evidence that the missions were indeed a US government deception, these corrupt government agencies now have to spend *six hours* to beat the truth down, point-by-point, even though they do so with obvious lies, sneaky misrepresentations, and the deliberate banning of available evidence and presenters which prove them wrong, all of which is simply further proof itself of the falsification of the Apollo Moon landings.

The above examples clearly show why there is so much censorship these days by all of the corrupt government-controlled media.

As lies eventually reveal themselves and cannot blossom forever, any more than a seed on concrete, the banning or censorship of contrary opinions, if they are truly "nonsense" as they claim, is entirely unnecessary, and only proves that they are truthful. Thusly, banning and censorship of information proves that what is being banned or censored would bring about necessary change that the evil forces who control the media and the world do not want.

Remember, this propagandized program's own description says, "One of America's greatest achievements is also one of its most controversial." If the Apollo missions were so *obviously real*, then they would be the *least* controversial event in history, rather than the *most*. This fact alone proves that there is another side of the story that is not being told, which many have already awakened to.

If there were just a *one-percent* chance that a politician, who the CIA disliked for exposing their corruption, was involved in a sex scandal, there would be thousands of journalists assigned to investigate and write about this remote possibility. *Supposedly* sunlit ninety-degree intersecting shadows from objects a few feet apart from one another, NASA's own Kelly Smith admitting that radiation protection beyond Earth orbit has *yet* to be invented, the fake photography of astronauts pretending to be halfway to the Moon while in low-Earth orbit, the revealing secret audio of the CIA prompting this radio delay deception, the privately recorded conversation of my threatened assassination by the CIA, the deliberate destruction of two hundred billion dollars worth of evidence, and only one-thousandth the capability of travel to the Moon fifty years later, certainly all together consists of at least a one percent or greater chance of a fraud (really a *one hundred percent* chance), and therefore merits some kind of journalistic investigation, yet no reporter in the entire world has ever been genuinely assigned to this task. **Why?** Simply because the exposing of this fraud would be the undoing of those who control the news media. Simple, right?

Seven different US networks, so far, have paid thousands of dollars for the exclusive license to broadcast the revealing NASA footage, only to be told at the eleventh hour *not to do it* by senior network executives, who are bedfellows with the CIA, whose criminality would be exposed if it were televised with a detailed explanation as to what it revealed. (Remember Carl Bernstein reported that the CIA's own documents disclosed that the CIA had at least 400 network executives and "journalists" working for them – and that was more than forty years ago when it was regulated ten times more than now.) The same thing happens in other countries as well. In the UK, the BBC likewise canceled its broadcast of *A Funny Thing Happened...* only three days before it's scheduled "surprise" telecast, even though they lost an enormous amount of money in the process. (I was privately informed that a senior United States government official personally telephoned the Director-General of the BBC and put pressure on the organization to not broadcast my documentary.) The executive producer of my film told me that he was even offered additional money to not publicize this reason for the BBC's cancellation.

None of this would be occurring if astronauts had *really* landed on the Moon. The reason why I am continually banned from speaking and showing my film is because four out of five people who watch my documentary with an open mind, reverse their opinion as to the authenticity of the missions. This is *precisely why* the government-controlled media outlets are so afraid to showcase the film, me, or *any* of my startling evidence of their highly criminal Moon landing deception!

Here is a typical comment from one of the people who purchased a DVD in order to watch my film *A Funny Thing Happened...*

Most moon hoax evidence is subjective. What is NOT subjective is the Apollo 11 astronauts on video staging the Earth shots by dimming the foreground of the TV camera and lying about the camera being right up against the round window to make it look like the Earth from one hundred thirty thousand miles away. This video IS damning. There is no reasonable explanation for this.
Dean

I was even banned, together with my film, from a major university after one of its private student clubs hired me to speak on this subject and show my movie. You would think that American colleges would be the most fertile ground for the open debate of the latest discoveries, yet the **exact opposite** is actually true. Just look at the word "*university*". In my opinion, it means "*universally conformed thinking*". "Institutions" are there to *institute* **conformity** of human thought, so that people who attend these institutes "of learning" (really *programming*) become "universal" in their thinking, and therefore are easier to control by those who run the world, who naturally, are the very ones who own and finance the universities!

This is truly what it means to be "institutionalized". In our upside-down world, you are really risking entering such "institutions" *sane* and leaving them *crazy*. These are the very same institutions whose own "scientists", in living memory, endorsed giving caffeine and sugar laden *Coca-Cola* to infants as a "healthy drink", and said that cigarettes were a "healthy" cure for a sore throat, when *in reality* the former gave children diabetes and the latter gave adults throat cancer! Additionally, the leading magazines, newspapers, and broadcast networks, also within living memory, the very ones who said that a contestant of an intelligence competition who received the answers in advance was "the smartest man in America", and that the questionable faked Moon landings were "real", published numerous endorsements for these highly destructive cigarettes, boasting in their publications and broadcasts hundreds of times that "*doctors* agree that they are *good* for you", when *in reality*, the **exact opposite** was true.

In living memory, these highly corrupt institutions, whose billionaires own nearly all of the media outlets in order to control public opinion (which is to make people believe the exact opposite of the truth), had nearly *half* of Americans and the people of the world smoking their "healthy" cigarettes, making more than a trillion dollars every thirty years from their sale. While these leaders of ours charged people this gigantic amount of money for the privilege of ending their lives prematurely and in much agony, they also profited in more trillions of dollars from the hospitals which they also own, charging ten thousand times more than the cost of cigarettes for treating people for the very suffering which they had just intentionally caused. In a world such as this, you can now see how the corrupt government agencies of the world would have no problem with the mere faking of a Moon television picture.

What other "health cures" of today are these genocidal entities not only *fabricating a market for*, yet also *deliberating creating a health crisis* for their own unscrupulous profiteering and dehumanizing agendas? If current dictatorial freedom-limiting laws are being so quickly implemented and naively obediently followed for the *alleged* reason of "public health", then why haven't the powers-that-be, if they are so concerned about the public's health, merely written a one sentence international law banning cigarettes, which are destined to kill **one billion people** in the next eighty years? This blatant contradiction means that theses recently imposed dictatorial laws are ***not*** for the **public's** benefit, rather they are for the benefit of those who **run the world**, so that they can better control the people of it.

"Each of you, for themself, by themself, and on their own responsibility, *must* speak. And it is a solemn and weighty responsibility, and not lightly to be flung aside at the bullying of pulpit, press, government, or the empty catchphrases of politicians. Each must, for themself alone, decide what is right and what is wrong, and which course is patriotic, and which isn't.

You cannot shirk this. To decide against your convictions is to be an unqualified and inexcusable traitor, both to yourself and to your country. Let them label you as they may. If you alone of all the nation shall decide one way, and that way be the right way according to your convictions of the right, you have done your duty by yourself and by your country. Hold up your head! You have nothing to be ashamed of."

– Mark Twain

Chapter Eleven
NASA's Greatest Fear

One important event in this already sad and alarming history is what is known as the "Apollo One Fire." At the request of one of my important sources, who was a spouse of an Apollo astronaut, I intentionally did not go into great detail in my film *A Funny Thing Happened...* about what I will finally share here. On January 27, 1967, all three members of the crew who were scheduled to be the first astronauts to perform a lunar landing were suddenly killed in an "accident." Without even igniting the engines of the rocket, just sitting in the spacecraft for a rehearsal, these three men were burned alive... *intentionally* as it turns out. According to my source, Betty Grissom, the widow of one of the murdered astronauts, this fire was set *deliberately*. Mrs. Grissom (who died in 2018) had asked me not to include the following information in my film, as she was pursuing her own legal action at the time and did not want any undue publicity generated by the premature disclosure of this information to interfere with that process. Betty Grissom was also one of several people directly involved in the Apollo program who asked me not to publicly divulge some highly significant information until after they have died, and for some of my sources, for even a longer specified duration after that. I am sharing some of this information here for the very first time.

Mrs. Grissom was absolutely convinced that the fire that killed her husband was set intentionally, yet she never understood why until I spoke with her. When I explained that I had uncovered undeniable proof that none of the Apollo crews ever went to the Moon, the association of the two events became crystal clear, as proof of the fraud, and proof that the Apollo One fire was intentional, have to be related to one another.

Not only was the wife of one of the deceased Apollo astronauts completely convinced that her husband was murdered by the CIA because of overwhelming evidence that she uncovered which proves this, and the family's investigation was exceedingly thorough, given their vested personal interest, that same astronaut's son Scott Grissom, a highly intelligent and skilled 747 pilot, also believes that the Apollo One fire was set deliberately. My belief is that Apollo astronaut Virgil "Gus" Grissom was targeted because of his lack of cooperation with the impending acts of deception, and for fear that he would disclose this secret to the American public and to the world.

According to Betty Grissom, her husband Virgil, who was commander of the Apollo One three-man crew, reported to her the day before he was murdered, that CIA agents were granted special access to the launch pad the previous day. **Why in the world would several CIA agents be at the launch pad right before the suspicious fire took place?** The answer is sadly obvious.

Virgil "Gus" Grissom, the man who *otherwise* would have been the first "man on the Moon", was by far the most publicly outspoken critic of the Apollo program. Mrs. Grissom told me that her husband informed her, just days before his death, that NASA astronauts were *at least* **ten years** away from landing a man on the Moon, *not* two years away as was their schedule, in order to keep President Kennedy's overly-ambitious goal at the time. Additionally, Virgil Grissom was in the process of writing an extensive and detailed report that was highly critical of the Apollo program, which he was planning to give to his United States Senator as soon as it was completed. Even more shocking than this, I was informed that CIA agents came to the Grissom household just minutes after Virgil's death and illegally confiscated this critical report, which somehow they knew about, and then abruptly left, **without even informing Betty at that time of her husband's recent demise.**

As uncovered in my extensive interviews about the Apollo

One fire with those closest to this homicidal tragedy, Apollo astronaut Virgil Grissom had decided to write his critical report for the Senator only as a last resort. He had, prior to this, repeatedly filed report after report with NASA, in exacting detail, as to the ineptitude of the Apollo program's hardware and operating procedures, citing over five hundred items that needed to be *immediately* fixed in order for their mission to succeed, yet not a *single* suggestion from the vehicle's own pilot was ever implemented, to Grissom's unbridled bewilderment. Grissom even appealed directly to the generals above him who were in charge of the Apollo project with his urgent concerns, yet all to no avail. This is because the high-ranking superiors at the Pentagon and the CIA already knew that they were either going to admit failure after Kennedy's unprecedented international boast to "put a man on the moon by the end of 1969", or more than likely, stage the missions to save face, and secretly spend the majority of the allotted billions of dollars on illegal, congressionally unsanctioned projects, such as the secret invasion of Cambodia and Laos. They obviously decided on the latter.

NASA had already achieved low-Earth orbit, and as this would be their perpetual limit anyway, this is exactly why they did not bother to expend further effort or expense to fix additional equipment that they knew they were not going to use. Instead, the money would be utilized for the Pentagon's secret and illegal projects, by charging the citizens of America, through their taxes, what would today be eighty million dollars each for things like a glorified electric golf cart, which they would cleverly rename as a "Moon Rover", naturally insisting that they were "indispensable". Not mentioning, of course, that if it broke down miles away from the lunar lander, which would not only prove the uselessness of the contraption to begin with, there was no guarantee that the beleaguered astronauts would not fall and seriously damage themselves and their spacesuits during their attempt to walk back to the LM, or die a painful death from oxygen deprivation in a beleaguered, yet failed attempt to do so.

It is my understanding that the CIA decided that the agency would postpone telling the Apollo astronauts of the coming deception for as long as possible, so that if something went wrong with their scheme beforehand, the smallest number of people would know about it. It was all of this which led to Grissom's perplexity as to why none of the faulty equipment designed to supposedly reach the Moon was being repaired or improved upon. Not only did Bill Kaysing, the science writer for Rocketdyne, say that he had seen and read a classified memorandum in which the rocket designer himself, Wernher von Braun, estimated the likelihood of a successful manned Moon mission at a mere *one in ten thousand chance*, Kaysing said that he personally eyewitnessed such incompetence at NASA, just as Grissom did, that he too thought that a successful manned lunar landing was decades, rather than two short years away.

Thomas Baron stated in both his written report, and in his congressional testimony, that many NAA engineers were slacking off at the launch site and that NASA did nothing to stop them drinking on the job. Bill Kaysing said that NASA employees were doing very little work most of the time, despite the pressing deadline, adding that entire departments were regularly forgotten about for months due to repeated grievous clerical errors and given no tasks at all, so their employees just sat around all day collecting high salaries forty hours a week for playing checkers and drinking alcohol. Witnessing this constant professional ineptitude with NASA contractors, along with all of their defective, untried equipment, both Kaysing and Grissom were continually baffled by the repeated outrageous and uniformed claim by NASA's public relations department that they were "completely on schedule to reach Kennedy's Moon goal by the end of 1969".

Apollo astronaut Virgil Grissom was so frustrated with the incompetence and lack of progress in the Moon landing program that he famously hung a large lemon on the spacecraft's entrance door just days before his death, indicating the vehicle's complete inadequacy to perform as required to reach the Moon.

The Apollo One crew (left to right, Ed White, Virgil "Gus" Grissom, and Roger Chaffee) expressing their concerns about their spacecraft's endless problems, who then presented this picture to Apollo project manager Joseph Shea on August 19, 1966, just five months before they would be killed with the same questionable equipment. NASA.

Additionally, and without NASA's permission, Grissom invited reporters in to take photographs of the lemon on top of the spacecraft, to be broadcast on national television, in order to publicly protest the repeated lie by NASA that they were on schedule for Kennedy's misspoken 1969 deadline. According to Kaysing, when one of the generals in charge of the project was eating his dinner at home that evening and saw Grissom's brazen disrespect for the chain of command on national television, going over his head to appeal directly to the American public for assistance, a decision was quickly made to eliminate the Apollo program's leading critic, who they feared would go public when he was eventually asked to participate in the upcoming Moon landing deception.

When Grissom's fellow Apollo astronauts saw his contempt for "the system", which had repeatedly failed them all, and his incredible forthrightness to do something about it, they all privately applauded him, yet no one besides Grissom dared to comment publicly about NASA's replete incompetence. According to my highly-credible sources closest to the Apollo program, all of the astronauts joked privately among themselves, that because of Grissom's dangerous stance against the powerful and unforgiving

NASA, they had better not stand too close to him, in case he was suddenly struck by lightning. The reason the Pentagon and the CIA decided to kill the other two crewmembers along with him, was simply so that it would not look like Grissom was being singled out, especially after his extremely recognizable public criticism of the Apollo program. Rather than being the targeted killing that it truly was, by killing two other men along with Grissom, this CIA contrived "accident" would instead appear to be an unfortunate happenstance. Utterly and completely despicable.

Grissom was frustrated with the dilapidated equipment right up until his death. The inept agency could not even get a simple wired intercom to work from the spacecraft to the next building. Among Grissom's last words were, "How are we going to get to the Moon when we can't talk between two buildings?" Moments later, Virgil Grissom, Edward White, and Roger Chaffee, all three with wives and young children, would be intentionally burned alive by their own corrupt government, for fear that one or more of them would not cooperate with the coming Moon landing deception, and in the process, as their protest against it, expose this horrible government corruption to the world.

This is what the US federal government and the CIA fears the most coming to light about the Apollo deception. Lying about going to the Moon, aside from it being an exemplary illustration of the federal government's and mankind's true depravity and juvenility, this deceitfulness *appears* to be mostly harmless – **until the government kills its own citizens in the process of covering it up.** Research reveals that a total of ten Apollo astronauts had mysterious, non-space-travel fatal "accidents" in just a three-year period leading up to the grand deception. These other men, like Grissom, were obviously people of high integrity, who also refused to cooperate with the Moon landing fakery after they were asked to, and were eliminated by their own government's agencies in order to keep this fraud a secret.

This, unfortunately, means that those who ascend to the highest offices of government power are generally those with the *least* amount of integrity, as those with the most integrity are eliminated by hook or crook from the corrupt leaders who are at the top. If this were not so, then Virgil Grissom, Edward White, and Roger Chaffee, along with President John Kennedy, would have died from old age rather than murder, and the Moon landings would still be a distant dream, rather than a despicable fraud. These corrupt people at the top of the world's unscrupulous governmental systems **are** the ones who are running our planet **right now**.

We should all be very fearful about this deadly predicament and immediately do something about it ... before it is too late.

Those astronauts who did participate in the falsified Moon missions, either for personal reward or from pressure, all became guilty parties nonetheless, and would thereby be obliged to keep this secret to their deaths, out of mutual self-preservation.

Imagine if ten employees of a single restaurant had mysterious fatal "accidents" all within a three-year period of one another. Would not the homicide detectives be all over the place looking for those responsible for their demise? Of course they would. Yet this same standard is not applied to the US federal government's murdered astronauts. Additionally, the Apollo program's second leading critic after Grissom, NASA mission quality inspector Thomas Baron, who was also a man of high integrity, and a meticulous record keeper, said that there was not a *single* NASA operating procedure, among *thousands*, that was completed without a compromising deviation from safety protocol. He also complained that all of the employees at NASA were constantly being shifted from one department to another, *just before* they had a full understanding of what they were doing, a very odd procedure that was the *precise opposite* of what you would do if you were *really* going to the Moon for the very first time.

Unbeknownst to Baron or Grissom, this perplexing order from above to constantly move workers to another department *right before* they became completely aware of the true technical challenges which laid ahead, was done so that no one at NASA ever saw the full picture of the inability of the equipment to actually reach the Moon. Everything was assumed, by trusting some other unseen division in the organization. This *departmentalization* was the same technique that was used during the construction of the highly secretive nuclear bomb during World War Two, which had nearly *one hundred and thirty thousand total employees*, with each one working on various minor parts, yet only about *eight* people at the very top knew what they were really building.

NASA whistleblower Bill Kaysing was one of the few who saw the whole picture, because he proofread and edited the spelling and grammar of leading official's texts in their classified memos, in order to not make them look like the illiterate people that some of them were (while others were not native English speakers, such as German scientists from the Nazi rocket programs). Kaysing had the highest of security clearances to be able to do this, as did Thomas Baron, which enabled them both to uniquely see what was *really* going on within NASA regarding the Apollo Moon landing program and its highly inexperienced contractors. When Baron, like Grissom, gradually became aware of the impossibility of them to reach the Moon, he too reported it in exacting detail to his superiors. Just like Grissom, Baron was completely ignored, as were his thousands of proposed important technical and safety changes, which he urgently recommended in written triplicate forms, that were unprecedentedly intentionally disregarded by his superiors, simply because the people at the very top knew that none of it would matter anyway, as they were going to secretly fake the Moon missions and only orbit the Earth at two hundred and fifty miles, a feat which they already had the workable equipment to accomplish.

When the Apollo One fire occurred on January 27, 1967, it was Thomas Baron, who worked in the quality control department of North American Aviation (NAA), that the United States Congress turned to for answers. NAA was subcontracted to NASA for the Apollo project and Baron had written a five hundred page report, which he submitted to Congress, containing detailed analysis of NASA's inability to reach the Moon in less than a *ten* year period, rather than the *two* years remaining in deceased Kennedy's naïve 1969 deadline. Just like the original videotapes, blueprints, and flight data from all of the Apollo missions, Baron's critical and comprehensive report of the severe inadequacies of the Moon landing program, mysteriously disappeared from the National Archives right after it was submitted to Congress.

The United States Congress even gave Baron highly respected "whistleblower status", because just prior to turning in his critical report of the Apollo program to Congress, Baron's employment was terminated by NAA, just days before the preplanned Apollo One fire, for having told the press that NASA's 1969 deadline was an impossibility. Baron had done so as a public protest of NASA and NAA's bewildering disinterest in fixing any of the inept Apollo equipment, just as Grissom had publicly protested with his lemon, because both of their superiors would not do a single thing about it, as they secretly knew they were not actually going to the Moon. Just like protesting Grissom, Baron too had a fatal "accident", only days before his next scheduled congressional testimony, in which Baron was planning to present an even more detailed and damaging report on NASA & NAA, something that the CIA was not about to allow to happen.

In order to get any available documentation at all about the Apollo One fire, the executive producer of my film paid ten thousand dollars to purchase a copy of the congressional report on the Apollo One fire (not the still missing Baron Report), from the estate of murdered Apollo astronaut Roger Chaffee. This document, like Baron's report, could not be found anywhere in government archives. When I read this report, I could see why.

In this rare document, that Roger Chaffee's widow had attained through her persistence decades ago, it was disclosed that the door to the capsule was intentionally changed, just before the fire, to one that illogically and unprecedentedly opened *inwardly*, rather than the standard *outward* design, suspiciously and significantly delaying their emergency escape once the CIA instigated fire started. The door was also originally ordered to remain open for the entire day of the crew's flight rehearsal, until an anonymous superior instructed that the door be closed and locked just before the fire. Additionally, a pile of rags, soaked in flammable liquid, was found right under Grissom's seat. **Unbelievable!**

This special report that I attained from the murdered Apollo astronaut's estate also reveals that NASA instruments recorded a mysterious and unexplainable dip in electrical power just prior to the fire. Mrs. Grissom told me that she suspected that some CIA espionage device had been tapped into the electrical system the previous day, which drew its power from the spacecraft, and that this foreign piece of sabotage equipment initiated the fire when it was activated, which simultaneously caused the observed and recorded unexplained dip in electrical power just before the fire. This is why her husband reported that the CIA was at NASA just two days before his murder, in order to covertly install their lethal piece of equipment into the spacecraft.

In an a not-so-clever mischievous attempt to supposedly "honor" the murdered astronauts, NASA and the CIA tried to "bury at sea" the Apollo One space capsule in which they died, which was really these agency's unlawful attempt to destroy all of the forensic evidence of the homicides that they had committed. Betty and Scott Grissom immediately filed a court injunction to stop this from happening, successfully arguing that important evidence still existed inside of the Apollo One spacecraft, which could indicate the *real* cause of the fire. Two more times NASA and the CIA tried to destroy the Apollo One space capsule with all the incriminating evidence therein, even falsely arguing decades later that they needed to disassemble it so that the parts could be used elsewhere – to save the taxpayers money! Coming from the organization that had no problem charging *eighty million dollars* for an electric golf cart supposedly to be used on the Moon, this criminal assertion is completely laughable. The Apollo One crew module remains out of public view and scrutiny to this day, in private storage at NASA's Langley Research Center, Virginia, not far from CIA headquarters. Only the door can be seen in a museum. Why would this be the case, unless NASA and the CIA were trying to conceal evidence of deliberate sabotage?

Virgil "Gus" Grissom was originally selected to be the "first man on the Moon" not only on account of his intelligence and aptitude, yet also because he had the best rapport with the media.

This was demonstrated during an early incident with the press in which Grissom displayed remarkable honesty, humor and humanity. In a previous solo Mercury flight, in what was named "Liberty Bell 7", when the spacecraft splashed down in the ocean, it had just been equipped with new explosive bolts on its door, in order to exit the capsule quickly in the event of an emergency. The intense impact of Grissom's spacecraft into the ocean caused these new explosive bolts to be triggered prematurely, which rapidly filled the capsule with water when it bobbed beneath sea level upon splashdown. Because of this, the spacecraft began to sink to the bottom of the ocean, taking Grissom along with it, with his spacesuit also beginning to fill with water, as he was foolishly instructed by NASA to remove his airtight helmet before exiting.

At the initially embarrassing press conference, Grissom explained that he had inadvertently added to his dilemma by having several bank rolls of nickels (five cent pieces) in his spacesuit's pockets, so that he could give these to his young son to hand out to his fellow classmates at his elementary school, as one-of-a-kind souvenirs which had "been in space". As the added weight had caused him to sink in the ocean all the more quickly, Grissom confessed to the reporters at his press conference that this turned out to be a rather bad idea, to which the members of the media laughed heartily along with him. When a reporter asked him if during the harrowing experience he was ever afraid, Grissom paused for a moment, then smiled and said, "Of course I was afraid," which further endeared the press and the public to him, by honestly revealing that all "heroes" share the same humanity as they do.

As the Apollo missions were really more of a publicity campaign than anything else, the federal government dearly wanted the first "man on the Moon" to be someone that the press and the public mutually adored. This is precisely the reason why they selected Virgil "Gus" Grissom for this monumental occasion. After he was killed, Neil Armstrong was moved up to replace Grissom because of his similar "all-American" image. Armstrong naïvely accepted, not yet informed of the impending great fraud that was fast approaching, of which he would be expected to participate.

When Armstrong was shortly thereafter asked to go along with the grand deception, I highly suspect that he initially turned down the offer, as he too, at least at that time in his life according to my research, was a man of high integrity. The only option left open to Armstrong at that point would be his highly publicized resignation from NASA, *after* he was already publicly chosen before the entire world to be the first "man on the Moon", something that would undoubtedly raise too much suspicion for the government's liking. As the CIA was not about to allow Armstrong to resign on the international stage after he had just been publicly chosen with such great accolades, the agency had to *compel* Armstrong to participate in their notorious crime.

Deductive reasoning suggests that the next step would be for the CIA to try to persuade Armstrong with an enticing bribe, because if he accepted under these terms, as I believe most of the other Apollo astronauts did, then he would be criminally complicit with them. I suspect, as man of principle that I believe he was *at that time*, that Armstrong declined their generous offer. Next, the CIA would have threatened his life, with the reminding of their murderous Apollo One fire to back up their threat. As Armstrong had been a test pilot for many years, charged with flying experimental aircraft that had never before been flown (a highly dangerous endeavor), I doubt if the threat of death meant much to him. After this, the heat would have to be turned up a bit more, and the lives of his wife and children would have been threatened next, as was done to the Security Chief at Cannon Air Force base where the first Moon landing was filmed, and even done to his surviving family member very recently. *This* is what I believe persuaded Armstrong to reluctantly cooperate with the CIA's criminal scheme, and why Armstrong did not want any pictures of himself standing on a fake moon film set for all of recorded history, which might eventually be exposed as one of the greatest deceptions of all time. This I believe, is also why Armstrong resigned from NASA shortly after his mission and subsequently rarely gave interviews, because the idea of continually lying for these despicable criminals turned his stomach sour.

I am not sure how many others were murderously eliminated in order to keep this historical government deceit a secret, yet it is the Apollo One fire that has them the most worried, should the truth about the Moon landing fraud come out publicly. It is certainly an incredibly deplorable thing for the United States government to have staged the Moon landings, yet it is beyond belief and completely outrageous in the eyes of history, and in the eyes of all humanity, to have brazenly and horrifically murdered their own citizens to cover it up, which they most certainly did.

Betty and Scott Grissom, who have investigated this matter more thoroughly than anyone else, are one **hundred percent certain** that the Apollo One fire was set *deliberately*, causing their husband and father to be callously burned alive. It would be an amazingly hard and bitter pill for the American public to swallow to finally realize that not only were they duped into believing that their most adored and heroic moment in United States history was a complete fraud, that on top of all this, their hard earned tax dollars were also used by their very own CIA to murder their neighbors, friends and family members in the process. The fact is, when the truth finally comes out about the falsified Moon missions, the Apollo One fire investigation will be immediately reopened, and the citizens of this country will also discover, to their even greater shock and dismay, that the government that they have for so long trusted, to whom they give a **third** of their paychecks for life, used their hard earned money to not only deceive them beyond belief about the Moon landings, yet to also exterminate their fellow countrymen, who dared expose their incredibly demonic corruption.

The US citizenry will be so alarmed and angry at their own government, that they will dismantle NASA and the agencies involved in all of this, and start all over. This is what the NBC news director rightly feared, and why he would not broadcast the incriminating Apollo 11 footage that I uncovered, even though he totally agreed that it conclusively proved the Moon landing fraud, as he did not want to be remembered for all time as the one to be singularly responsible for such a dramatic shift in world history.

My argument to him was the same as my repeated motto to myself during this entire unprecedented and bizarre adventure, "If the truth of government corruption causes its collapse, then the truth is doing its intended job."

The first document of the United States, the Declaration of Independence, was written as a result of a tyrannical government (the United Kingdom) murdering and stealing from the citizens under their care. It was asserted, in writing for all the world to see, that as equal persons on planet Earth, we are all entitled to:

> Life, liberty and the pursuit of happiness. That to secure these rights, governments are instituted among men, deriving their just powers from the consent of the governed, that whenever any form of government becomes *destructive of these ends, it is the right of the people to alter or to abolish it.* [emphasis added]

The murdering of their own citizens, Virgil "Gus" Grissom, Edward White and Roger Chaffee, among many others, to keep the federal government's Moon landing fraud from being exposed, is this same government's **stealing** the **right of life** from its own citizens, as the Declaration of Independence states is the very reason that entitles the citizens to *abolish* such a corrupt government.

This inevitable paradigm shift away from the monstrously immoral governmental systems which currently overlord humanity, as the Apollo deception disclosure would undoubtedly cause, is NASA's, the federal government's, and the CIA's biggest fear, and why, as exposed in *Astronauts Gone Wild*, they will all fight to the death to keep this crime of theirs a secret for as long as they possibly can.

"Have I become your enemy for telling you the truth?"

– *Galatians 4:16*

Chapter Twelve

How to Get Out of This Mess

A merican author Ellen G. White once said, "Our condemnation in The Judgment will not result from the fact that we have been in error, but from the fact that we have neglected heaven-sent opportunities for learning what is Truth."

The fact remains, and I will repeat it as often as necessary until the horrible truth finally sinks in, if *all* of the scientists from *all* of the nations of the world, even with fifty years more advanced space and computer technology, cannot go to the Moon today, and if NASA can now only send its astronauts *one thousandth* the distance to the Moon, it means, plain and simple, that they certainly did not walk on the Moon with untried antiquated 1960s technology on the very first try. Period.

Technology does not go backwards. All of these facts eventually become obvious to anyone with an open mind, who does not have a religious attachment to the blasphemous event.

Just as a gangster's children would have a hard time seeing dear old papa as anything but a benevolent patriarch, prideful intellectuals, as well as deceived citizens, will seldom admit, without being forcibly shown, that their idolized science and aggrandized leaders can be just as corrupt as a pedophile priest.

Furthermore, if putting a man on the Moon is supposed to be the greatest achievement of mankind, then certainly not doing so, lying about it to the entire world and murdering their own workers to cover it up, is what is **really** one of the most profound events in human history. This is why the *falsification* of the Apollo missions is more profound historically than if they had *actually* gone.

Thusly, this great truth, as to the *true* depraved nature of humanity and their corruptive governments, the deceptive, arrogant, and criminal nature thereof, is being withheld from the majority of the people of the world by the highly criminal individuals at the top, because they are the ones who committed the Moon landing fraud, and the revealing of it would bring their rule to an end. You can see now why these evil forces, under threat of their own extinction, are continually belittling those who expose their deception, through their otherwise needless hundreds of videos, news stories, and websites, solely created to defend the Moon landing lie, because the exposure of it will most certainly bring about their own demise.

Now you understand my earnest devout passion, as a true patriot of America, to expose this horrendous crime against not only the people of the United States, yet also against the rest of the people of the world, and to recorded history itself, in order to usher in the most needed betterment of mankind, as the revealing of the Moon landing deception would inevitably bring, and without the revealing of which, our collective intellectual and moral growth will be forever destroyed.

The old saying "give them an inch and they'll take a mile" is so very true about the United States federal government and governments in general. Power is addictive and insatiable, therefore *ever-increasing*. When government becomes so deeply entrenched in such an institutionalized criminal manner, as it is today with no end in sight, those of noble character tend to flee its ranks to private life to escape its immorality, leaving a vacuum in these high places for unscrupulous opportunists, who no longer defend the justice of the individual, instead supporting the corruptive system, which helped them get elected for this very purpose.

A reading of the American constitution would amaze most citizens with its supreme simplicity of verbiage. All of the monumental foundational laws which initially governed the entire United States of America, and all of the individual freedoms acknowledged therein through the Declaration of Independence, amounted to only four pages, with the most far reaching laws of the Constitution generally consisting of only one to three sentences, such as:

> Congress shall make no law respecting an establishment
> of religion, or prohibiting the free exercise thereof; or
> abridging the freedom of speech, or of the press; or the
> right of the people peaceably to assemble, and to petition
> the Government for a redress of grievances.

You see here that the foundational laws of freedom of religion, freedom of speech, and freedom of journalists, was written in just one sentence. This utter simplicity is wonderfully amazing, especially when today the average corrupt billion-dollar-corporation-inspired "laws" that are passed, just for the favorable regulation of a single commodity of theirs, amount to at least fifteen pages, with some exceeding more than one thousand pages, detailing to the minutest degree possible, every selfish advantage written specifically for their liking of its authors.

The "free press" spoken of in this *foundational* United States law is especially worth noting, as the current form of *supposed* "news media" is not independent at all. As self-seeking corporations and the criminal CIA owns ninety-nine percent of the market share of media outlets, which naturally promote their own corrupt agendas while highly suppressing those who expose them, then the "news" can hardly be *free* and *independent*, now can it? What this really means is that corporation and CIA-owned news media is a violation of law, or *illegal*, as the press is supposed to be free, that is *neutral and independent of influence*. The only way that a country can have a *neutral and independent of influence* press is if it is *also* "of the people, by the people, and for the people." The question is, how can the news media become this?

The only way that I can see for the news media to be *genuinely independent of influence* is for it to become a nonprofit entity of the people. As the war in Iraq cost one billion dollars a day while it lasted three times longer than World War Two, I think, for the good of the country, that there should be about a billion dollars a month allocated (only twelve billion dollars a year out of a nearly five thousand billion dollar annual budget) to support a completely new methodology for getting the *actual* truth of what is going on in America and the world to its people, especially after the current system has proven to be so disastrously corrupt with its *intentional* concealment of facts from their own citizens, as so aptly proven by the Moon landing deception.

Members of the press should be chosen by lottery. All radio and TV stations should be required by law to provide the necessary technical equipment, as well as two daily one-hour time slots for news broadcasts from this newly formed non-profit, publicly run, news entity. All magazines and similar publications should be required by law to provide ten percent of their space for this "Free Press Co-op", while making corporate and government news reporting illegal. The twelve billion dollar annual budget can pay for the salaries of those involved. All of this should immediately help to stifle rampant corporate and government lies, which have been used so grievously to take advantage of their own people and to rob them of the truth which they rightly deserve.

While we're on the subject of a lottery system, the constitution, and overhauling the corrupt federal government, a look at this world's very first democracy is in order. It was founded in Greece about two thousand five hundred years ago. Take a wild guess as to how their leaders were selected. It was an incredibly fair system, which had an amazing built-in safeguard against systemic corruption. The representatives of their legislatures were chosen **by lottery**, just like a jury of your peers. If we allow the life or death decision of a capital crime to be decided by people who are chosen by lottery, then I think the decision as to whether or not put the label "Contains GMOs" on a bottle of ketchup can be decided in the same manner. Without elections, there is no corrupt influence of them, no corrupt favors to pay back for corrupt money given to corrupt people to win them, and no millions of hours of time and billions of dollars wasted to conduct them, all of which will be much better spent benefiting the public directly.

There should be a **one**-term *lifetime limit* for **all** public offices at federal, state, and local levels, which could be set at a five-year term. All executive offices, such as president, governor and mayor, can be nominated by these lottery-elected legislatures from among their own membership. Five candidates for these executive offices can then be chosen by nomination and voting by these lottery-elected representatives, for the public to then vote on by majority, after these candidates for executive offices publicly debate three times. The top two candidates of the five can then debate three more times, after which they can be chosen by public majority vote in a final general election, without any outside financing allowed, and with the newly formed "Non-profit Free Press Co-op" being required to give each candidate the exact same about of time and questions.

I think it is about time that we utilized the common sense of teachers, artisans and small business owners, as a safeguard against corrupt corporate and CIA takeovers. Before criminal dictators and politicians eventually overtook this highly respected Greek system of original democracy, it worked so well that it lasted **five hundred years**. We cannot just fine tune or make adjustments to a corrupt system, we need to build an entirely **new one** from scratch. What have we got to lose except more fake Moon landings, more assassinated presidents, and Americans incapacitated from even being able to truthfully label the ingredients inside of their own ketchup, much less having any influence whatsoever to stop an immoral overseas war which needlessly kill members of their own family. If a public official ever says that they will not do something, and then does it, or attempts to do it (such as raising taxes), or says that they will do something, and then does not do it, or start to do it within one year (like building a bridge they promised to build), then that person should be immediately terminated from duty and incarcerated. Lies from our government representatives need to be punished as severely as crimes. It is ridiculous that we allow our leaders to perpetually lie to us and break promises without any accountability whatsoever.

In my opinion, even in a functioning "of the people" government (which we no longer have), there should be a "constitutional convention" of representatives every ten years, which
regularly re-establishes the simplicity of the laws of the Founding
Fathers and Mothers, thusly trimming back, rather than adding
to, the canon of established law, as with fewer rules there is more
freedom. Lobbying either needs to be outlawed, or completely
regulated in fairness, with equal opportunity for everyone from
all side of an argument to do so, with all of the conversations
thereabout being publicly recorded for future posterity and
present review. All "gifts" whatsoever to public representatives
need to be outlawed for their entire lifetimes. (Why any gifts
to representatives are presently allowed in the current system,
only further proves its criminality.) Heads of government agencies, like the FBI, EPA, and the Justice Department, need to be
elected from their own membership, instead of by biased and
corruptible presidential appointments. Finally, as the congress
and senate had no say whatsoever in the faking of the Moon
landings, then whoever *actually* controls the United States government today in such a despotic manner to have made these
highly criminal decisions (I believe the CIA), will then have to
be decisively eliminated.

You must do this investigation of the truth and much-
needed world changing yourself, because these institutionalized
criminals have very smartly bought up all of the mainstream
media to control your thoughts and your emotions, and thereby
your actions, specifically so that you will not do this. If you
do not start this restoration of justice now, then you will be
perpetually sleepwalking though these government gangster's
hypnotic manipulation into fatal oblivion. Once awakened from
their intoxicating trance of celebrity-politics-sports-disaster fed
media, it is then becomes your responsibility to wake up others,
and then for everyone to immediately do something about it.

To be quite honest, it seems like a hopeless uphill battle
against a tidal wave of unstoppable evil. It will take **Divine
Intervention** and *repentant fervent prayer* for it to be otherwise.

Please join with me in regularly beseeching our Eternal Creator to *directly intervene* to put an end to this unspeakable government depravity, or do whatever you morally can to stop it, before this thick fog of wickedness fatally consumes the helpless victims of America and the world, who are naïvely treating their criminal overlords as heroic liberators, when in fact they are secretly being enslaved by them for all of Eternity.

"The Truth will set you Free."

– John 8:32

Sibrel.com *Moon Man* link **#15**

Acknowledgements

I would like to thank the people who helped reveal this sad deception that the United States government so arrogantly perpetrated on their own people, all the while using their hard earned tax dollars to do so.

First, my thanks go to the late William (Bill) Kaysing, who worked on the Apollo program at Rocketdyne, for his years of grandfatherly patience with me until I finally accepted that my beloved Moon landings were indeed falsified.

Secondly, G.S., whose moral and financial support for this investigation began before anyone else's, long before I was as certain of this grandiose deception.

Thirdly, the anonymous Executive Producer of A Funny Thing Happened on the Way to the Moon and Astronauts Gone Wild, whose friendship and sense of humor helped me persevere though the perilous times of this investigation, which meant more to me than his patriotic financial sacrifice to bring this despicable action of our country into the light.

Fourthly, my friends Brugh, Corbin, Mike, John, Robert, Jarrah, Brett, Seb, Jackie, Bobby, and Dan, as well as numerous others, who kept reminding me that my findings were absolutely true and that this peculiar revelation was indeed historically and spiritually important enough to have invested all of my many years of passion exposing it.

Fifthly, to those behind-the-scenes astronauts and their family members, who admitted to me privately that the Moon missions were indeed falsified, and who helped in covert ways to reveal this important truth.

Sixthly, to the numerous present and past military and governmental officials, who are not corrupt, who have repeatedly saved my and my sources' lives, provided invaluable information, and risked their own lives to reveal this existing sad state of affairs of our fallen nation and world, in order to make them better.

Seventhly, to my loving loyal wife, who persevered throughout this bizarre and difficult project.

Notes

1. Letter from John Adams to Abigail Adams, April 26, 1777.

2. "The average American spends 24 hours a week online", *MIT Technology Review*, https://www.technologyreview.com/2018/01/23/146069/the-average-american-spends-24-hours-a-week-online, accessed May 2021.
And "U.S. Adults now spend nearly 6 hours per day watching video", Tech Crunch, https://techcrunch.com/2018/07/31/u-s-adults-now-spend-nearly-6-hours-per-day-watching-video, accessed May 2021.

3. There is a percentage of cannibalism within the Mantis population in nature but it is not systemic, it is dependent on circumstances. "Mantids and Cannibalism: A Surprisingly Complicated Affair", https://askentomologists.com/2015/03/23/mantids-and-cannibalism, accessed May 2021.

4. NASA administrator James Webb's surprise resignation on October 7, 1968, was ostensibly due to LBJ's March 1968 announcement that he was not going to stand for re-election, so Webb was stepping back in order that the next President choose his own administrator. Three discrepancies: 1) Webb later told the Washington Post that LBJ had told him of his discussion, privately in *July 1967.* 2) At a change of White House administration, NASA administrators generally leave their posts on or shortly after, *inauguration day in late January.* 3) On October 7, 1968, with the election on November 5th, no one knew with absolute certainty who would be the next President, or whether he would require the NASA administrator to leave. Robert Seaman of NASA records that in August 1968 while abroad with Webb at a conference, Webb learned that NASA's Thomas Paine and his colleagues had taken the decision to launch Apollo 8 in December. Webb had asked him what he thought of the decision and Seaman had replied that it was hasty and ill advised. Fifty-two years later, in May 2019 there was a repeat performance, when NASA's chief of human spaceflight, Doug Loverro, after only six months in the job, suddenly resigned just eight days ahead, of the first NASA launch of humans to LEO in nine years. At the time Loverro declined to elaborate on the specifics of his resignation, only stating that it was not associated with the crew launch to the ISS but that it was relative to the Artemis lunar lander contracts. *The Washington Post,* https://www.washingtonpost.com/archive/lifestyle/1981/09/24/james-webb-and-nasas-reach-for-the-moon/253a284e-bdd9-480f-ae0b-19a96ca7d961, accessed May 2021.

And "NASA's chief of human spaceflight resigns on cusp of critical crew launch", https://spaceflightnow.com/2020/05/19/nasas-chief-of-human-space-flight-resigns-on-cusp-of-critical-crew-launch, accessed May 2021.
And "Here's why NASA's chief of human spaceflight resigned – and why it matters", arstechnica.com/science/2020/05/heres-why-nasas-chief-of-human-spaceflight-resigned-and-why-it-matters, accessed May 2021.

5. Extracts from *Plain Speaking an Oral Biography of Harry. S. Truman.* G. P. Putnam's Sons, New York, 1974 ISBN 0425026647.

6. The CIA and Google – "How the CIA made Google" https://medium.com/insurge-intelligence/how-the-cia-made-google-e836451a959e
And "Google's true origin partly lies in CIA and NSA research grants for mass surveillance" https://qz.com/1145669/googles-true-origin-partly-lies-in-cia-and-nsa-research-grants-for-mass-surveillance/
And Forbes Report: "CIA Secretly Owned Global Encryption Provider, Built Backdoors, Spied On 100+ Foreign Governments" https://www.forbes.com/sites/daveywinder/2020/02/12/cia-secretly-bought-global-encryption-provider-built-backdoors-spied-on-100-foreign-governments/?sh=48474bb9580a, accessed May 2021.

7. "America's Missing Money: The federal government can't account for $21 trillion – but does anybody care", https://www.city-journal.org/html/americas-missing-money-15725.html, accessed May 2021.

8. The CIA and the Media. After leaving *The Washington Post* in 1977, Carl Bernstein spent six months looking at the relationship of the CIA and the press during the Cold War years. His 25,000-word cover story, "How Americas Most Powerful News Media Worked Hand in Glove with the Central Intelligence Agency and Why the Church Committee Covered It Up", published in *RollingStone* on October 20, 1977, important, http://www.carlbernstein.com/magazine_cia_and_media.php.

9. DARPA Source for 10 Second Delay in All TV/Radio Transmissions. The source is a confidential Pentagon Technology Official & NPR Transmission Engineer. This fact can be tested: Broadcast of WWV (Fort Collins Standard Time) *vs* when a "News" program commences. Exactly 10 seconds different), https://www.time.gov, accessed May 2021.

10. "Every challenge astronauts will face on a flight to Mars", https://

phys.org/news/2021-02-astronauts-flight-mars.html, accessed May 2021.
And "Living in Space", European Space Agency, https://www.esa.int/
Enabling_Support/Preparing_for_the_Future/Discovery_and_Preparation/
Living_in_space, accessed May 2021.
And "Robots vs. Humans: Who Should Explore Space?" https://www.scienti-
ficamerican.com/article/robots-vs-humans-who-should-explore, accessed May
2021.

11. Bill Clinton *My Life* Hutchinson/ Knopf Publishing Group, 2004.

12. The Van Allen belts. At the time of Apollo little knowledge about these
belts was available. However, nature was doing what it does, and these belts
were equally complex and as active back in 1960s as we find them today. We
just did not have anything near to the required technology available today, and
we still do not know all that much about them. Research on the belts using the two
The Van Allen probes in 2012, "Van Allen Radiation Belts: Facts & Findings"
https://www.space.com/33948-van-allen-radiation-belts.html, accessed May
2021.
And "Measuring Radiation" https://www.nrc.gov/about-nrc/radiation/
health-effects/measuring-radiation.html, accessed May 2021.
And "Traveling in Space Features: Keeping Astronauts Healthy", https://www.
nasa.gov/vision/space/travelinginspace/keeping_astronauts_healthy.html,
accessed May 2021.
And referencing radiation effects in LEO: Fuglesang C, Narici L, Picozza P,
Sannita WG. *Phosphenes in low-Earth orbit: survey responses from 59 astronauts,*
Aviat Space Environ Med 2006; 77:449–452.
As for radiation on the lunar surface, a 2008 study from the Colorado school
of Mines concerning lunar outposts has this to say: "The cosmic radiation on
the moon poses a real danger to astronauts and equipment on the lunar surface... The lunar astronauts can expect to encounter high energy, high speed,
and high damage GCR"... Without a shielding mechanism to block the hazardous radiation present on the lunar surface however, extended manned stays on
the moon are not possible. "Extended Lunar Outpost Radiation Shielding",
https://spacegrant.colorado.edu/COSGC_Projects/symposium_
archive/2008/papers/S08_14%20Extended%20Lunar%20Outpost%20
Radiation%20Shielding.pdf, accessed May 2021.

13. Mark S. Robinson Professor, School of Earth and Space Exploration
Arizona State University, Tempe, AZ, principal investigator for LROC.

14. Standard Chinese Curriculum: *Moon Landings False*. The author heard the question on the game show "Hollywood Squares" (and presumed, because it was a national game show, that the question was researched) "True or False: Does China Teach in its universities that the American Moon Landings were faked?" "Answer: True."
And China has 2,600+ universities "Number of public colleges and universities in China between 2009 and 2019", https://www.statista.com/statistics/226982/number-of-universities-in-china, accessed May 2021.

15. "Who has Walked on the Moon?" https://solarsystem.nasa.gov/news/890/who-has-walked-on-the-moon, accessed May 2021.

16. Extracted from *Wikipedia* on the subject of the Apollo Moon Fraud.

17. In 1962 prior to any retro-reflectors being placed on the Moon, Scientists Louis Smullin and Giorgio Fiocco at MIT (Massachusetts Institute of Technology) succeeded in their laser ranging observation. Soviet scientists at the Crimean Astrophysical Observatory repeated the experiment later that same year. LROC: http://science.nasa.gov/headlines.
And For some very informative data on the imaging of the Apollo sites, this article from 2005, "Abandoned Spaceships", http://web.archive.org/web/20090808020433/http://science.nasa.gov/headlines/y2005/11jul_lroc.htm, accessed May 2021.

18. Dr James Van Allen 1958 – see Sibrel.com *Moon Man* link #9B.

19. Wernher Von Braun, Willy Ley, Dr. Fred Whipple, *Conquest of the Moon*, Viking Press, New York 1953.

20. Statement by Dick Nafzger at a news conference in 2009.

21. In the 2007 documentary, introduced by Ron Howard, the film clips of lunar activity sourced from VHS recordings and used several times, albeit greatly reduced within the screen size to minimize their low quality, still reveal visible "tracking" line problems at the bottom of the images.
The document written by John Sarkissian, then the Operations Scientist at CSIRO Parkes Observatory, is a must read for the background on these lost recordings "The Search for the Apollo 11 SSTV Tapes" https://www.parkes.atnf.csiro.au/news_events/apollo11/The_Apollo11_SSTV_Tapes_Search.pdf, accessed May 2021.

And NASA's version of events can be found here: "Not-Unsolved Mysteries: The 'Lost' Apollo 11 Tapes", https://www.nasa.gov/feature/not-unsolved-mysteries-the-lost-apollo-11-tapes, accessed May 2021.

And for Eugene Krantz's comment concerning the Disassembled Tape Machines, watch Aron Ranen's film, Apollo 11 Flight Director Gene Kranz Admits important Apollo 11 Science and Video Tapes are misssing, https://www.youtube.com/watch?v=-5YQ_ey5508, accessed May 2021.

And "Wow! Apollo 11 Moon Walk Videotapes from NASA Sold at Sotheby's", https://thehotbid.com/2019/07/23/wow-those-apollo-11-moon-walk-video-tapes-from-nasa-sold-at-sothebys-for-scroll-down-to-see, accessed May 2021.

And This reference also refers to Richard Hoagland's assertions that these missing tapes were 'lost' because of his findings concerning lunar artifacts such as 'the shard', "Lunar Anomalies", https://www.tarrdaniel.com/documents/Ufology/lunar_anomaly.html, accessed May 2021.

22. The point stands, but since that section was written some change did occur. "In the summer of 2016 Congress passed a bill that was subsequently signed by President Obama. This legislation establishes a federal standard for labeling foods that have been made with genetically modified organisms. The bill requires food manufacturers to use one of three types of labels to inform consumers when GMO ingredients are in their products: a statement on the package, directions to a website or a phone number, or a QR code "What's the story on GMOs and labeling?" https://ag.purdue.edu/GMOs/Pages/GMOsandLabels.aspx, accessed May 2021.

Printed in the USA
CPSIA information can be obtained
at www.ICGtesting.com
LVHW022234151123
764091LV00033B/808

9 781513 686561